Content & Language Integrated Learning

JN088911

Shigeru Sasajima

Satsuki Kojima

Yukiko Abe

Motoki Sato

Barry Kavanagh

Taizo Kudo

SDGs

Sustainable Development Goals

SUSTAINABLE DEVELOPMENT GOALS

SANSHUSHA

はじめに

　本教科書は、CLIL（Content and Language Integrated Learning）（内容と言語を統合した学習）という教育理念を基盤として構成してあります。内容（題材）として、国際連合（国連）が設定し、世界中が注目している持続可能な開発目標（SDGs）を扱います。高校や大学などで日本語で学ぶSDGsに英語を統合し、英語コミュニケーション能力を育成できるように工夫しました。さらに、SDGsに実践的にかかわる専門家、英語文法の専門家など、異なる分野でCLIL教育を実践的に推進する著者が作成に携わりました。

　CLILは、内容（Content）、思考（Cognition）、コミュニケーション（Communication）、文化間理解（Culture）という、「4つのC」（4Cs）を考慮して学ぶことを大切にしています。本教科書はSDGsの理解と実践を目標としています。そのために英語は必要なツールです。英語を使うためには語彙、文法、発音という基礎は疎かにできません。そこで、文法学習にも焦点を当てています。SDGsの様々な場面で英語を実践として活用するための「文法の基礎」を強調しています。基本のルールを活用して語彙を増やし、実践的にSDGsを理解し、不完全であっても英語を使いながら「意味を伝える（communicate）」活動をすることを大切にしています。この「4つのC」（4Cs）を常に頭に置き活動しながら、SDGsの17の目標を少しでも達成できるような基礎的な英語コミュニケーション力を育成することが、本教科書の目的です。

　学習者の英語力は、CEFRの6レベルのB1（一部B2）を想定していますが、リスニングとスピーキングについては、A2程度で十分学習可能な内容です。学習者によっては多少むずかしい部分もありますが、英語の難易度にしばられることなく、内容にこだわり、積極的に活動し、教科書の話題から多様に興味を広げ自律的に学んでください。本教科書での学習を通じて、持続可能な開発目標（SDGs）を理解した「グローバル市民（Global citizen）」として活躍することを願います。

　　　　　　　　　　　　　　　　　　　　　　　　　　　　　　　　　　　　著者一同

各 Unit の構成と活動

各 Unit で学ぶ SDG を提示

1 Background (facts & figures) ——— Unit に関連する数字や事実の確認

2 Topic-related vocabulary check ——— 関連する語句の確認

  2.1 Listen and fill in the blanks ——— 語句の発音と意味の理解

  2.2 Ask each other in pairs ——— 語句の意味を使いながら確認

3 Knowledge check (quiz) ——— Unit に関連する知識の確認

  3.1 Look up the answer online ——— 予習などで調べて答えを見つける

  3.2 Do some research online and discuss the following questions with your classmates
——— 学んだ知識をさらに発展して調べ、話し合う（日本語も可）

4 Understanding SDGs ——— SDGs の理解

  4.1 Listen and fill in the blanks ——— 聞いて読んで事実を理解する

  4.2 Questions for discussion ——— 事実をもとに考える

5 Reading ——— Unit に関連する話題

  5.1 Question ——— 話題を読み取るポイントを考える

  5.2 Discussion points ——— 話題を深く考える（日本語も可）

6 Basic grammar exercises ——— 文法の復習（英語使用のため）

  6.1 Quiz ——— 文法の基本の復習

  6.2 Read aloud ——— 文法に注意しながら音読

  6.3 Discussion ——— 文法に注意しながら内容を考える

7 Reading graphs and charts ——— 文法の実際の使用を理解

8 Research ——— Unit で学んだことを総合してリサーチして発表

・グロサリー

・文法マスター（文法理解のために基礎練習）

持続可能な開発目標（SDGs）とは？

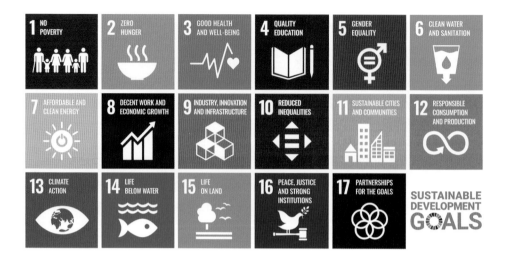

　持続可能な開発目標は、Sustainable Developmental Goals の略で、SDGs と言われます。SDGs は、国連が設定した 2016 年から 2030 年までの国際社会の共通目標です。「質の高い教育（quality education）」「ジェンダー平等（gender equality）」「気候変動へのアクション（climate action）」など、世界が一丸となって取り組む必要がある 17 の目標（goal）と 169 のターゲット（target）で構成されています。

　2000 年 9 月にニューヨークの国連本部で国連ミレニアム・サミットが開催されました。その際に、参加した 147 の国家元首を含む 189 の国連加盟国代表が、「国連ミレニアム宣言」を採択し、21 世紀の国際社会の目標として、より安全で豊かな世界づくりへの協力を約束しました。この宣言と 1990 年代に開催された主要な国際会議やサミットでの開発目標をまとめたものが、「ミレニアム開発目標（MDGs）」（Millennium Development Goals）です。その発展として SDGs が設定されました。

　作成にあたっては、世界各地でのテーマ別の会合、国別の会合、オンライン調査、聞き取り調査などで「みんなの」意見を聞きました。その結果、2015 年 9 月の国連サミットで全会一致により採択されました。「グローバル・ゴールズ（Global Goals）」とも呼ばれています。貧困を半減するなどの平均値での目標ではなく、SDGs は「誰一人取り残さない（No one left behind）」という理念のもと、貧困ゼロ、飢餓ゼロと、世界中のすべての人が「理想の社会」にたどり着くことを目標としています。

世界人口は増え続け、1950 年当時の 25 億人から、2020 年には 77 億人、2060 年には 100 億人を超えると推定されています。人口が増え続ければ、その分、経済社会活動も活発になり、CO_2 の排出量、水の消費量、車の数、魚の漁獲量の増加など地球や環境への負担が高まります。世界で開発が進み、各国が豊かになるのは喜ばしい反面、世界中のすべての国が日本のような暮らしをすると、地球が 2.8 個、アメリカのような生活では 5 個、カタールのような生活では 8.8 個が必要です。

　国家の枠組みを超えたテロ組織や新型コロナウィルスのような感染症など、新たな脅威も生まれています。つまり、「これまで問題なく生活できたからこれからも同じ生き方でよい」ではなく、個人も組織も、新しい生き方やあり方を考えなくてはいけない時期にきているのです。

　SDGs を知り、学ぶことは、「グローバル市民（global citizen）」として、地球、世界の課題を「自分事」として捉える視点やマインドを持つきっかけにもなります。SDGs を考えることは、今の世代だけではなく、次の世代、続いていくその先の世代のことも意識し、持続可能な未来をつくっていく責任感にもつながります。現在、世界の教育現場で、SDGs は積極的に紹介され、SDGs に貢献できる人材育成（グローバル教育）が行われています。

　もう一つ忘れてはいけないことは、英語という言語の重要性です。日本語やそれぞれの国の言語も大切ですが、互いのコミュニケーションを考えるとやはり英語が最も便利な言語です。英語で SDGs の内容を共有し、互いの文化を理解し、それぞれ個人で自律的に考え、意見を述べ、コミュニケーションできることが求められます。この教科書『CLIL 英語で考える SDGs』は、そのことを目的としています。学習者が、SDGs を知識として学ぶのではなく、SDGs を英語で理解し行動するために活用し、世界で活躍することを期待します。

　SDGs に関してはインターネット上に多くのリソースがあります。詳しくはそれぞれで参照してください。例を一つあげておきます。

17 Goals to Transform Our World

https://www.un.org/sustainabledevelopment/

CONTENTS

Unit 1

No Poverty/ Zero Hunger
貧困をなくそう・飢餓をゼロに

現在形

SDGs 1,2

Unit 2

Good Health and Well-Being
すべての人に健康と福祉を

接続詞

SDG 3

Unit 3

Quality Education
質の高い教育をみんなに

現在進行形

SDG 4

Unit 4

Gender Equality/ Reduced Inequalities
ジェンダー平等を実現しよう・人や国の不平等をなくそう

過去形・過去進行形

SDGs 5,10

Unit 5

Clean Water and Sanitation
安全な水とトイレを世界中に

助動詞

SDG 6

Unit 6

Affordable and Clean Energy
エネルギーをみんなにそしてクリーンに

形容詞・副詞

SDG 7

Unit 7

Decent Work and Economic Growth
働きがいも経済成長も

分詞

SDG 8

Unit 1

No Poverty / Zero Hunger
貧困をなくそう・飢餓をゼロに

Goal 1 End poverty in all its forms everywhere
Goal 2 End hunger, achieve food security and improved nutrition and promote sustainable agriculture

1 Background (facts & figures)

Which facts and figures are you interested in?

- **About 10 % of the world population** still live in extreme poverty, surviving on **less than 1.9 US dollars a day**.
- **Two thirds of undernourished people** worldwide live in sub-Saharan Africa and southern Asia.

2 Topic-related vocabulary check

CD 001
↓ 001

2.1 Listen and fill in the blanks

words	meaning
poverty *n.*	the state of being extremely (　　　　　) [＝貧しい]
undernourished *adj.*	unhealthy and weak due to not enough (　　　　　) [＝食事]
obese *adj.*	very (　　　　) in a way that is unhealthy [＝太っている]
eradicate *v.*	to completely (　　　　) rid of something such as a disease or a social problem [＝排除する]
sanitation *n.*	the protection of public (　　　　) by removing and treating waste, etc. [＝健康]
underweight *n.*	weighing (　　　　) than is expected or normal [＝より少ない]
disaster *n.*	a sudden event such as a flood or storm which causes great (　　　　) [＝損害・被害]
malnutrition *n.*	lack of proper (　　　　) [＝栄養]
stunted *adj.*	not (　　　　) properly to full size [＝発育する]
orphanage *n.*	a large house where (　　　　) who are orphans live and are taken care of [＝子供たち]

2.2 Ask each other in pairs

    A: What does "poverty" mean? Please explain it to me.

    B: "Poverty" means the state of being extremely poor.

3 Knowledge check (quiz)

3.1 Look up the answer online

1) How many people live with less than 1.9 US dollars a day?

   a) Around 700 people.

   b) Around 7,000 people.

   c) Over 700 million people.

2) How many children under 5 in the world are obese?

   a) About 4 million.

   b) About 40 million.

   c) About 400 million.

3) Are there more people living in poverty now, compared to 25 years ago?

   a) Yes, there are. There are more than one billion people living in poverty.

   b) No, there aren't. About one billion people have been lifted out of poverty.

4) What is the percentage of deaths due to disaster in low- and middle-income countries?

   a) More than 50 %.

   b) More than 90 %.

5) What percentage of employed workers and their families worldwide are extremely poor?

   a) 2 %.   b) 8 %.   c) 15 %.

3.2 Do some research online and discuss the following questions with your classmates

1) Do you think it is important to provide economic support for poverty? Is there any other idea to eradicate poverty?

   e.g. Sure. I think some financial support for poor countries is necessary, but we need to know how they are used and where they go. It is important to know the facts.

2) Do you think there is a relationship between poverty and obesity?

   e.g. Yes. I did some research on poverty and obesity. The fact is that many people in poor countries actually have problems with obesity. It surprised me.

©Lorrie Graham

4.1 Listen and fill in the blanks

CD 002
↓ 002

Goal 1 End poverty in all its forms everywhere

- Eradicating extreme (¹   ) is one of the crucial issues in the world. The number of people living in extreme poverty declined by more than (²   ) between 1990 and (³   ), but still one person in every (⁴   ) is extremely poor. Half of all people living in poverty are under (⁵   ) years old. Those people lack food, clean (⁶   ) water, sanitation, medical care and education.
- Disasters can often lead to a (⁷   ) in economic development and make poverty (⁸   ). It is estimated that disasters resulted in more than 3 trillion dollars of direct economic (⁹   ) from 1998 to 2017. Moreover, 1.3 million people (¹⁰   ) from climate-related disasters.

CD 003
↓ 003

Goal 2 End hunger, achieve food security and improved nutrition and promote sustainable agriculture

- Unfortunately, extreme hunger and malnutrition in the world (¹¹   ) about 821 million people in 2017. And also, (¹²   ) million children under five suffered from stunting and 49 million children were (¹³   ). These people were hungry and undernourished due to (¹⁴   ) degradation, conflict and drought. The number of undernourished people has been on the (¹⁵   ) since 2014 from 784 million people. On the other hand, 40 million children under 5 years of age were overweight in 2018.
- In order to end (¹⁶   ) and malnutrition, it is crucial to support (¹⁷   ) farmers, create equal access to land, develop technology and markets, and encourage sustainable (¹⁸   ). It is also necessary to help develop agriculture in (¹⁹   ) countries. To improve agricultural productivity, we will need to have international (²⁰   ) to establish investment in infrastructure and technology.

4.2 Questions for discussion

1) What do you think about extreme poverty?
2) Why are there still too many undernourished people in the world?
3) What can we do to end hunger and malnutrition?
4) Do you think people in your country suffer from hunger?

5.1 Do you know about food banks? Are there any food banks in Japan?

Even though there are over 700 million people living without enough food in the world, more than one third of food produced is disposed of every year for various reasons, such as damaged packaging. In fact, those foods are still edible and safe. The amount of food loss in Japan is substantial compared to the total amount of food aid distributed world-wide.

Food banks are one of the solutions for food loss. Food banks <u>collect</u> surplus food and <u>distribute</u> it to those who need food support, such as orphanages, women's shelters,

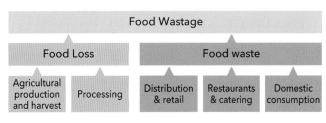

welfare agencies, NPOs and community centers. Food banking has many advantages not only for donors but also for beneficiaries. Donors, including food manufacturers, food importers and farmers, can reduce their disposal costs. They can also distribute free samples to recipient agencies to promote their products. Since donating is a corporate social responsibility (CSR), donors can also make an impact on the community. Beneficiaries can reduce food expenses and save money as well. They can also eat nutritious food and also enjoy some premium snacks or newly released sweets that they could not normally afford to buy.

Second Harvest Japan is the first food bank in Japan. Since it started its activities in 2002, the amount of deliveries grew from 30 tons to 3,152 tons in 2012. This is an increase of over 100 times. To support its activities, we need to donate food and money. We can also donate our time to help them as a volunteer.

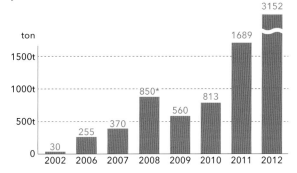

Food Delivery 2002-2012
*In 2008 we received a one-time donation of 320 tons of tomato juice

Source: Second Harvest Japan

5.2 Discussion points

1) Why is a third of food produced in the world wasted? Do you waste food?
2) Do you understand the system of the food bank? Do you think it is good?
3) Do you want to be a beneficiary?
4) What can we do to support Second Harvest Japan's activities?

Grammar point　present simple（現在形）

文中の下線部 collect と distribute は事実を述べているので現在形で表されます。現在形は、習慣、状態、真理などを述べるときに使われます。（➡文法マスター参照）

e.g. People in developing countries **need** food support.

6 Basic grammar exercises: present simple

6.1 Choose the appropriate answer

1) Some girls in developing nations (are usually waking / usually wake) up early to collect water.
2) Disasters (often create / are often creating) an impact on communities.
3) I (know / am knowing) one of the leading food manufactures.
4) Food banks (are usually correcting / usually correct) the surplus food problem.
5) Many people who live in extreme poverty (are needing / need) financial support.

6.2 Read aloud the text and see how the present simple is used

Two out of three adults that live in the U.S. are reported to be overweight or obese. However, the rise of obesity is limited to a few countries. These include most developed countries and some developing countries. Some poor people in developing countries, who don't usually have regular meals but mostly fast food, are liable to suffer from obesity.

6.3 Discussion: Do you eat fast food often? Are you worried about obesity?

7 Reading graphs and charts

Check how the present simple is used and discuss the topic of hunger in groups

THE CYCLE OF HUNGER

There are many ways hunger can trap people in a cycle of poverty and need. Here is how it can burden someone for a lifetime, and pass it on to the next generation.

MERCY CORPS

CHILDREN
Poor nutrition stunts physical and mental development

YOUTH
Chronic health problems keep kids out of school

FAMILY
Poor health during pregnancy leads to an undernourished child—*starting the cycle again*

ADULTS
A lack of education limits the ability to work

POOR NUTRITION · HEALTH PROBLEMS · INABILITY TO WORK · UNHEALTHY PREGNANCIES

https://www.mercycorps.org/blog/quick-facts-global-hunger

8 Research

Try to do some research and make a presentation using slides, a poster or a handout

🆃🅸🅿🆂 for doing your research

1) Define the term(s), such as poverty, hunger, food bank or food loss
2) Identify the problems of poverty and hunger that SDG 1 and SDG 2 show
3) Examine the realities around you with regards to SDG 1 and SDG 2
4) Check the local or global efforts that are being done to achieve SDG 1 and SDG 2
5) Explain what you can do to achieve SDG 1 and SDG 2
6) Refer to the local policies that aim to solve the problems of poverty and hunger
7) Propose your own ideas or actions to solve these problems

Sample

Let's start a food bank

Sanshu Hana
CLIL University

1

SDGs 1 & 2

•Goal 1: End poverty in all
its forms everywhere
•Goal 2: End hunger, achieve
food security and
improved nutrition
and promote
sustainable agriculture

2

What are food banks?

• Food banks collect surplus food and distribute it to those who need food support.
• Orphanages, women's shelters, welfare agencies, NPOs and community centers.
• Food banking has many advantages.

3

Second harvest Japan

• **Second Harvest Japan** is the food bank in Japan.
• To support its activities, we need to donate and raise money.
We can also donate our time to help people as a volunteer.

4

Problems and Realities

• **Food waste** is food loss that occurs "at the end of the food chain"
• **Food loss** is "the decrease in edible food mass throughout the part of the supply chain"

5

Our ideas or actions to solve the problems

• Don't waste food!
• Stop food loss!
• Understand food banking!
• Let's create a food bank in our city!
• If we do so, we can achieve the SDGs 1 & 2.

6

Unit 2 Good Health and Well-Being

すべての人に健康と福祉を

Goal 3 Ensure healthy lives and promote well-being for all at all ages

1 Background (facts & figures)

Which facts and figures are you interested in?

- **More than five million children** die before their fifth birthday each year.
- Unsafe water, inadequate sanitation, and lack of hygiene led to **a total of 870,000 deaths** in 2016.

©UN-Photo

2 Topic-related vocabulary check

2.1 Listen and fill in the blanks

words	meaning
mortality *n.*	the number of (　　　　　) in a particular society during a particular period of time ［= 死亡者］
fatal *adj.*	causing death or (　　　　　) effects ［= 悪い］
facility *n.*	a (　　　　　), equipment, and service used for a particular purpose or activity ［= 建物］
preventable *adj.*	capable of being stopped from (　　　　　) ［= 起こる］
hygienic *adj.*	(　　　　　) in order to prevent disease ［= 清潔な］
infectious *adj.*	able to be passed (　　　　　) person to person ［= 〜から］
disease *n.*	an illness that affects people, often caused by (　　　　　) ［= 感染］
contribute *v.*	to be one of the (　　　　　) of something ［= 原因］

2.2 Ask each other in pairs

A: What does "mortality" mean? Please explain it to me.

B: "Mortality" is the number of deaths in a particular society during a particular period of time.

3.1 Look up the answer online

1) Are children under 5 years of age likely to survive today than in 2000?

©UN-Photo

a) Yes, they are. The total number of under-5 deaths dropped from 9.8 million in 2000 to 5.4 million in 2017.

b) No, they aren't. More than 9 million children still die each year.

2) What is the second leading cause of death among people aged 15 to 29 globally?
   a) HIV.
   b) Suicide.
   c) Drugs and alcohol.

3) Vaccinations resulted in an 80 % drop in death from _____.
   a) HIV
   b) measles
   c) malaria

©UN-Photo

4) Two thirds of the world's maternal deaths occur in sub-Saharan Africa. In these regions, _____ percent of births were assisted by skilled attendants.
   a) 20
   b) 40
   c) 60

©UN-Photo

3.2 Do some research online and discuss the following questions with your classmates

1) How do you prevent illness and diseases every day?
   e.g. I avoid junk food and have a good sleep.

2) Do you think there is a relationship between poverty and well-being?
   e.g. Yes. I did research regarding poverty and well-being. I found out that many people in poor countries actually die prematurely.

©UN-Photo

4.1 Listen and fill in the blanks

Goal 3 Ensure healthy lives and promote well-being for all at all ages

Reproductive, maternal, newborn and child health

- Millions of children are more likely to (¹   ) today than in 2000, but more than 5 million children still die before reaching (²   ) years of age. (³   ) of those deaths occurred in sub-Saharan Africa and another (⁴   ) percent in Southern Asia. Almost half of the total number of under-5 deaths took place in the first (⁵   ) of life.

- Nearly 300,000 women around the world died due to complications in (⁶   ) and childbirth in 2017. Over (⁷   ) percent of these deaths occurred in low- and middle-income countries, and two thirds of them were in sub-Saharan Africa. In sub-Saharan Africa, only (⁸   ) percent of births were assisted by skilled (⁹   ). These deaths are (¹⁰   ) with appropriate management and care. Globally in 2018, (¹¹   ) percent of all births took place in the presence of skilled health personnel.

Environmental risk

- Unsafe drinking water, inadequate sanitation and lack of hygiene continue to be (¹²   ) contributors to global mortality, resulting in 870,000 deaths in 2016. Air pollution increases the risk of (¹³   ). Household air pollution, mainly due to polluting fuels and technologies for cooking, led to around 4 million deaths in 2016, and (¹⁴   ) air pollution from traffic, industry, power-generation, waste-burning and residential fuel combustion resulted in around 4.2 million deaths in 2016.

Mental health

- Mental (¹⁵   ) occur in all regions and cultures. The most common are anxiety and depression. These can frequently lead to (¹⁶   ). In 2012, an estimated 800,000 people worldwide committed suicide. Globally, suicide is the second (¹⁷   ) cause of death among people aged between (¹⁸   ) and (¹⁹   ).

4.2 Questions for discussion

1) What health problem are you interested in?
2) Do you know the life expectancy in your country or hometown?
3) Why are there still too many children dying in the world?
4) What can be done to improve mental health in your country?

5.1 Why do we need to wash our hands? When and how do you wash your hands?

About 16,000 children under the age of 5 are dying from preventable diseases such as diarrhea and pneumonia every day in developing countries, <u>and</u> most of the diseases that cause death are preventable through the simple act of handwashing with soap.

SARAYA Co., Ltd., which developed the first medicated hand soap and dispenser in Japan, started the "Wash A Million Hands!" project in 2010. The project aims to educate people in Uganda on correct handwashing using soap to prevent children from fatal diseases. Conflict in the country has lasted over 20 years, and since 2006, Uganda has lacked infrastructure such as water supplying facilities, schools, and health centers. Due to poor hygienic conditions, only 14 % of people washed their hands after using the toilet in 2007.

WHO HAS THE LEAST ACCESS?

The world's least developed countries have the least access to handwashing facilities. In 2015:

27%
of the population had basic handwashing facilities.

26%
had handwashing facilities lacking soap or water

47%
had no facilities at all.

15% Only 15 % of the population in sub-Saharan African had access to basic handwashing facilities with soap and water in 2015.

https://www.unicef.org/stories/infographic-get-facts-handwashing

SARAYA has built handwashing facilities <u>and</u> offered support for hygienic education to children and their mothers. The rate of people who wash their hands with soap after going to the toilet increased to 37 % in 2017. <u>In addition</u>, the under-5 mortality rate in Uganda decreased from 89 to 53 deaths per 1,000 live births between 2009 and 2016.

The project has shown great results, <u>but</u> the hygienic environment in Uganda is still severe. The under-5 mortality rate in Uganda remains at 55 deaths per 1,000 live births, which is a bit higher than the SDGs target of 45 deaths per 1,000 live births. To achieve the SDGs target, we further need to raise awareness of handwashing practice <u>and</u> educate people on its importance to the world and future generations.

5.2 Discussion points

1) How is diarrhea and pneumonia preventable?
2) What is the purpose of the "Wash A Million Hands!" project?
3) Do you wash your hands after going to the toilet? Have you ever seen people who don't do it?
4) Do you think handwashing activities save children's lives?

Grammar point　conjunctions（接続詞）

文中の下線部 and, but, in addition は、語句と語句、文と文などを結びつける接続詞です。接続詞の代わりに also, on the other hand, therefore などを使うこともできます。（➡文法マスター参照）

e.g. Some people have no basic healthcare **and** others lack social protection.

---

6 | Basic grammar exercises: conjunctions

6.1 Choose the appropriate answer

1) I don't drink (and / or / but) smoke for my well-being.

2) Most people want to have a healthy, safe (and / or / but) comfortable life.

3) We did great work, (and / or / but) the environment is not good enough yet.

6.2 Read aloud the text and see how conjunctions are used

Millions of children are more likely to survive today than before. However, 5 million children or more still die before they reach the age of five. Moreover, half of those deaths occurred in sub-Saharan Africa and thirty percent occurred in Southern Asia. Therefore, we should consider the problem seriously.

6.3 Discussion: Why is handwashing essential to prevent child deaths? Give as many reasons as you can.

---

7 | Reading graphs and charts

Check how conjunctions are used and discuss newborn deaths in groups

Newborn deaths account for 45 % of deaths among children under the age of 5 globally. In addition, 2.6 million babies die in the last 3 months of pregnancy or during stillbirths, and 303,000 maternal deaths occur each year. We could prevent at least two-thirds of these deaths, and that is one of the aims of the global 'Every Newborn Action Plan' (ENAP) that launched in 2014. It provides a road map of strategic actions for ending preventable newborn mortality and stillbirths, and contributes to reducing maternal mortality and morbidity.

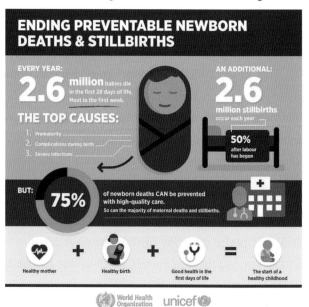

8 Research

Try to do some research and make a presentation using slides, a poster or a handout

for doing your research

1) Define the term(s), such as good health and well-being
2) Identify the problems of healthy lives and well-being that SDG 3 shows
3) Examine the realities around you with regard to SDG 3
4) Check the local or global efforts that are being done to achieve SDG 3
5) Explain what you can do to achieve SDG 3
6) Refer to the local policies that aim to solve the problems of health and well-being
7) Propose your own ideas or actions to solve these problems

Sample

PROTECT MORE PEOPLE FROM TABACCO

CLIL University
Sanshu Hana

1

Outline

1. Health Effects
2. Data and Statistics
3. Youth Tobacco Prevention
4. Global Tabacco Control
5. Conclusion

2

Smoking can cause cancer almost anywhere in your body

3

Youth are exposed to E-cigarette advertisements

retail stores   the Internet   TV or movies   magazines

4

Youth Tobacco

In 2013, more than a quarter million middle school and high school students never smoked regular cigarettes but had used e-cigarettes. 3 times as many as 2011

Source:
Office on Smoking and Health National Center for Chronic Disease Prevention and Health Promotion

5

What the government needs to do

- monitor tobacco use and prevention policies
- protect people from tobacco smoke
- offer help people to quit tobacco use
- warn people about the dangers of tobacco
- enforce bans on tobacco advertising promotion, and sponsorship
- raise taxes on tobacco

Source: World Health Organization

6

Unit 3

Quality Education

質の高い教育をみんなに

Goal 4 Ensure inclusive and equitable quality education and promote lifelong learning opportunities for all

---

1 Background (facts & figures)

Which facts and figures are you interested in?

- **617 million children and adolescents lack** minimum proficiency in reading and mathematics.
- **750 million adults** still remain illiterate.
- **1 out of 5 children, adolescents and youth** between 6 and 17 years old are not attending school.

---

2 Topic-related vocabulary check

CD 008
↓ 008

2.1 Listen and fill in the blanks

words	meaning
education *n.*	the process of teaching and ( ), usually at school [= 学び]
proficiency *n.*	a good standard of ( ), experience and skill [= 能力]
illiterate *adj.*	not having the basic ability to ( ) and write [= 読む]
early childhood education *n.*	( ) and other forms of education provided for children before entering primary school [= 幼稚園]
compulsory *adj.*	( ) by the law or authority [= 必要な]
enrolment rate *n.*	the rate of ( ) who have arranged to join a school, university, course, etc. [= 学生・生徒]
literacy rate *n.*	the rate of people who can read and ( ) [= 書く]
remote education *n.*	the education of students who study online at ( ) [= 家]

2.2 Ask each other in pairs

A: What does "illiterate" mean? Please explain it to me.

B: "Illiterate" means not having the basic ability to read and write.

3 Knowledge check (quiz)

3.1 Look up the answer online

1) Non-proficiency rates are the highest in _____, where 88 percent of children of primary and lower secondary school age were not proficient in reading in 2015.
   a) South Asia
   b) Latin America
   c) sub-Saharan Africa

2) In 2016, only _____% of children experienced early childhood education (kindergartens, nursery schools, etc.) in the least developed countries (LDCs).
   a) 43   b) 53   c) 63

3) Although considerable progress in educational participation has been seen since 2000, _____ million children, adolescents and youth (6 to 17 years old) were still out of school in 2017.
   a) 62   b) 262   c) 462

4) In the LDCs, there are many teachers who have not received good teacher training before starting to teach. In 2017, the percentage of trained teachers in secondary education in sub-Saharan African countries was _____%.
   a) 50   b) 65   c) 80

5) About _____ of all illiterate people in the world were women in 2016.
   a) one half   b) two thirds   c) three quarters

3.2 Do some research online and discuss the following questions with your classmates

1) Are there any school-age children who don't go to school?
   e.g. Not in Japan, but I saw some in a country I visited last summer.

2) What prevents children from going to school?
   e.g. I guess some parents have their children stay home to help them work or do household chores.

4.1 Listen and fill in the blanks

> **Goal 4** Ensure inclusive and equitable quality education and promote lifelong learning opportunities for all

- Education is the key to realizing sustainable development of human society. Without education, it is very difficult for us to develop our own societies, break from the cycle of (1   ), reduce (2   ), and foster (3   ) of cultural differences.
- Education can be divided into levels. (4   ) education, usually for children of about 6 to 12 years old, is provided at primary or elementary school. The next level of education is called (5   ) education, which is for 12 to 15-year-old students as part of (6   ) education in some countries, while it is offered as an option in other countries. After finishing secondary education, many people in developed countries receive tertiary education, which is (7   ) at places such as colleges and universities.
- Education is a process of teaching and learning what society has established. Thus, the contents taught through education may (8   ) from country to country. For example, Japanese secondary schools provide Japanese martial arts classes as part of (9   ) courses, while British secondary schools provide (10   ) education for all students.
- In some countries, many schools lack basic resources such as electricity, water, computers, and the Internet. In 2017, 90 % of schools in the world had access to electricity and 84 % to drinking water; in sub-Saharan African countries, only (11   ) % of schools had electricity and (12   ) % had drinking water. As for information and communication technologies, only (13   ) of sub-Saharan African schools had access to the Internet.

4.2 Questions for discussion

1) Do you think everyone should participate in early childhood education before entering a primary or elementary school? Why or why not?
2) Do you think senior high schools should be compulsory? Why or why not?
3) Do you think the enrolment rate of tertiary education should be higher in Japan?
4) Who do you think should pay for education?

5.1 Do you know why there are so many children who don't go to school?

If you live in Japan, you may not be surprised to hear that the enrolment rate at primary education in Japan is nearly 100 %. When you look at the data of enrolment rates in other countries, however, you may be surprised at how low the rate is in some countries. According to the data issued by the UNESCO Institute for Statistics (UIS), the rates of out-of-school children of primary school age in 2018 were 47.35 % in Eritrea, 37.89 % in Djibouti, and 24.71 % in Pakistan. In terms of regions, the highest rate was found in sub-Saharan African countries.

Actually, there are some very serious reasons why so many children don't go to school.

- **Lack of schools:** There are no schools they can attend near their home. It is very tough for small children to walk for hours, which may deprive them of energy and motivation for studying.
- **Lack of teachers:** Even if there is a school building, there are few teachers present. Lack of teachers is mainly due to lack of teacher training, low payment for teachers, and bad school environments.
- **Lack of money:** In many countries compulsory education is basically free of charge, but school children need some money for textbooks and stationery. Their parents are also not rich enough to pay for them.
- **Child labor:** Instead of going to school, children have to work for their household because their parents' income is low, their parents are sick, or there are no adults who can take care of them.
- **Parents' attitude toward education:** Some parents consider education less important than work. They sometimes don't allow girls to go to school.

5.2 Discussion points

1) Where are Eritrea, Djibouti, and Pakistan on the map?
2) Why is the salary for teachers very low in some countries?
3) Suppose you are a first-year elementary school student, and you have to walk to school. How many kilometers is the maximum distance you could walk from your house to school?
4) What are the main reasons why many children don't go to school in Eritrea, Djibouti, and Pakistan?

Grammar point　present progressive（現在進行形）

現在進行形（be + -ing）は、進行中の動作や継続（〜している（ところだ））、確実な未来（これから〜する）、状況や物事の変化（〜している、しつつある）」などの表現ができます。（➡文法マスター参照）
　　e.g. Some NGOs **are building** schools in Cambodia.

6 Basic grammar exercises: present progressive

6.1 Choose the appropriate answer

1) One out of five children, adolescents and youth between 6 and 17 years old (do not attend / are not attending) school now.

2) Look at the picture on the right. The girl (carries / is carrying) water with a big bucket.

3) Only 13 people (works / are working) as teachers in Niue.

6.2 Read aloud the text and see how the present progressive is used

Education is changing in the world. Many countries have developed remote education systems. Students can study online at home using PCs, tablets or smartphones. Even in developing countries such as Kenya and Tanzania, the governments are making efforts to develop online education systems.

6.3 Discussion: Do you agree with the idea that the Japanese government should invest more in education? Why or why not?

7 Reading graphs and charts

Check how the present progressive is used and discuss education in groups

In the U.S., tablets are becoming popular among students these days. The rate of parents who planned to purchase tablets for their kids rose 5 % from 2013 to 2014, while laptops declined slightly from 25 to 21 percent. Probably more and more parents in Japan are also planning to buy tablets for their children now.

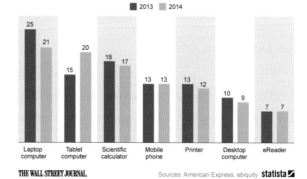

https://www.statista.com/chart/2620/back-to-school-shopping/

8 Research

Try to do some research and make a presentation using slides, a poster or a handout

🇹🇮🇵🇸 for doing your research

1) Define the term(s), such as (quality) education, proficiency, and minimum literacy
2) Identify the problems of education that SDG 4 shows
3) Examine the realities around you with regards to SDG 4
4) Check the local or global efforts that are being done to achieve SDG 4
5) Explain what you can do to achieve SDG 4
6) Refer to the local government policies that aim to solve the problems of education
7) Propose your own ideas or actions to solve these problems

Sample

Helping students from overseas

Sanshu Hana
CLIL University

1

Elementary students from overseas in the city

愛知県内の外国人児童数

| | | | 8758 | 9562 |
| 6676 | 7327 | 8023 | | |

6676 7327 8023 8758 9562

2015   2016   2017   2018   2019

2

Problems in daily life

- Cultural differences

- Expenses

- Language (Parents / children)

3

Students from overseas: Their problems at school

- Learning support
  - Local government
  - Community
  - Peers

- Basic literacy
- Bullying

4

Assistance for students from overseas: Language support

- For students
  - Textbooks / handouts
  - Assistants
- For parents
  - Handouts / Web pages
- Japanese language schools / teaching volunteers

5

Assistance for students from overseas: Community building

- At school
  - Crosscultural understanding
  - Education on human rights

- In the community
  - Events
  - Working together
  - Volunteer activities

6

Unit 4 — Gender Equality / Reduced Inequalities

ジェンダー平等を実現しよう／人や国の不平等をなくそう

Goal 5 Achieve gender equality and empower all women and girls

Goal 10 Reduce inequality within and among countries

1 Background (facts & figures)

Which facts and figures are you interested in?

- Women devote on average **roughly three times more hours a day** to unpaid care and domestic work than men.

- Up to **30 percent of income inequality** is due to inequality within households, including between women and men.

©UN-Photo

2 Topic-related vocabulary check

CD 011
↓ 011

2.1 Listen and fill in the blanks

words	meaning
gender *n.*	the state of being male, female, or neuter as expressed by social or ( ) distinctions and differences [＝文化的な]
decision-making *n.*	the process of making important ( ) [＝決定]
unpaid work *n.*	work ( ) receiving a salary, wage or payment [＝～なしで]
discrimination *n.*	treating a person or group differently from another in an ( ) way [＝不公平な]
socio-economic *adj.*	involving both ( ) and economic aspects [＝社会的な]
duty-free *n.*	goods that you can buy or bring into a country without paying ( ) on them [＝税]
migrant *n.*	someone who goes to live in another area or country, especially in order to find ( ) [＝仕事]
well-being *n.*	the state of being ( ) and happy [＝健康な]

2.2 Ask each other in pairs

A: What does "gender" mean? Please explain it to me.

B: "Gender" means the state of being male, female, or neuter as expressed by social or cultural distinctions and differences.

3 Knowledge check (quiz)

3.1 Look up the answer online

1) What percentage of ever-partnered women and girls aged 15 to 49 years have experienced physical and/or sexual partner violence in a year?
   a) 3 %.　b) 18 %.　c) 35 %.

©Yuichi Ishida

2) Twenty percent of women aged 20 to 24 years were married _____.
   a) after 18 years old　b) before 18 years old

3) Women continue to be underrepresented at all levels of political leadership. As of January 2019, women's representation in national parliaments stood at _____ on average.
   a) 24.3 %　b) 10.5 %　c) 45 %

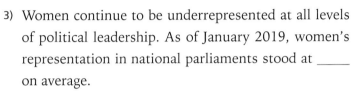
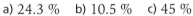

©Avalon／時事通信フォト

4) Nearly two thirds of the world's 781 million illiterate adults are women. Girls are still less likely to be enrolled in school than boys in the past two decades. Women account for _____ of the world's illiterate people.
   a) 34 %　b) 56 %　c) 64 %

5) Women are paid _____ less than men for comparable work across all regions and sectors in the world. At the current rate of progress, it will take 170 years to close the pay gap.
   a) 24 %　b) 48 %　c) 70 %

3.2 Do some research online and discuss the following questions with your classmates

1) Do you think it is important to increase women's leadership? Do you have any ideas on how to change the situation?
   e.g. Yes. I believe that women's representation in leadership is very important.

2) What are the LDCs? Why do we need to offer special assistance and treatment to the LDCs?
   e.g. The LDCs or the least developed countries are low-income, low-developed and vulnerable countries. They have severe problems in sustainable development.

4.1 Listen and fill in the blanks

CD 012
↓ 012

Goal 5 Achieve gender equality and empower all women and girls

- Gender equality is a basic human (¹   ), and its achievement has enormous socio-economic influences. Empowering women fuels growing economies, driving up (²   ) and growth. Yet (³   ) inequalities remain deeply stable in every society. Many women can't easily (⁴   ) decent work, and frequently face work segregation and gender wage gaps. They can often be blocked access to (⁵   ) education and health care. Women all over the world can suffer from (⁶   ) and discrimination.

- Women are under-represented in political and economic (⁷   ) processes. The United Nations has made significant progress in advancing gender equality for many years, (⁸   ) landmark agreements (⁹   ) as the Convention on the Elimination of All Forms of Discrimination (¹⁰   ) Women (CEDAW).

CD 013
↓ 013

Goal 10 Reduce inequality within and among countries

- We can't control economic (¹¹   ). In 2019, the world's 2,153 billionaires had more wealth than 4.6 (¹²   ) people. This disparity is based on the current economic system that values the (¹³   ) of the rich (¹⁴   ), which is more than a large amount of hours of the most (¹⁵   ) work done primarily by women and (¹⁶   ) around the world.

- In developing countries, cooking, cleaning, and fetching water and firewood are essential (¹⁷   ) tasks for the well-being of societies, communities and the functioning of the economy. The heavy and (¹⁸   ) responsibility of care work creates a lot more gender and economic inequalities.

Source: Report of Time to Care by Oxfam

4.2 Questions for discussion
1) Which SDG are you interested in, Goal 5 or Goal 10?
2) Why do we need to eliminate all forms of harmful practices, such as child, early and forced marriage and female genital mutilation (FGM)?
3) What kind of social system or protection do we need to achieve greater equality?
4) Do you think people in your country suffer from inequality? Why?

5.1 Why did Shabana study in a secret school? What is the power of education?

Under the Taliban regime in Afghanistan girls' education was forbidden. Shabana Basij-Rasikh <u>dressed</u> as a boy and <u>went</u> to a secret school with her older sister in Kabul during her childhood. It <u>was</u> the only way that girls <u>could</u> study. Each day, they <u>took</u> different ways to school so that no one <u>could</u> suspect their activities. Their parents <u>believed</u> in the power of education.

Shabana sometimes <u>felt</u> scared to go to the secret school. She <u>was crying</u> and asking her father not to send her to school, but he <u>said</u> to her, "You can lose everything you own in your life. Your money can be stolen. But the one thing that will always remain with you is what is in here. Your education is the biggest investment in your life. Don't ever regret it."

Shabana is now the President of the School of Leadership, Afghanistan (SOLA). It is an Afghanistan-led first private boarding school to provide education opportunities and security for girls. After the Taliban regime was driven out, she co-founded SOLA in 2008, when she <u>was</u> 18 years old. It <u>mitigated</u> the risks in traveling to and from school daily. She hopes girls will be critical thinkers and leaders to shape their nation's future.

Still in Afghanistan, nearly 3 million girls are out of school. 33 % of girls married before the age of 18, and 63 % of them are illiterate. However, she continues to make efforts toward girls' education and empowerment, because she believes she can change the world by educating girls. As an educator, humanitarian, and women's right activist, she gives students and society a new view of what is possible.

5.2 Discussion points

1) Why did Shabana study in a secret school with her sister during the Taliban regime in Afghanistan?
2) Why did she ask her parents not to send her to the secret school?
3) What did her father think about her education?
4) Discuss the current situation of girls' education in Afghanistan.

文中の下線部 **dressed** や **went** は動詞の過去形（-ed）で、過去の状態や動作を表します。**was crying** は過去進行形で、過去のある時点で進行していた動作や継続していた状態を表します。（➡文法マスター参照）

e.g. While boys **were enjoying** school life, girls in some countries **had** to work.

6 Basic grammar exercises: past simple and past progressive

6.1 Choose the appropriate answer

1) A lack of education (was leading / led) to devastating effects on girls some years ago.

2) Her father (was listening / listened) to the radio when she entered his room.

3) The Taliban (was prohibiting / prohibited) education for girls twenty years ago.

4) She (was deciding / decided) to fight against inequality last year.

6.2 Read aloud the text and see how the past simple and the past progressive are used

SDG 5 aims to end child marriage. Historically many girls were suffering from fear of child marriage. I heard a sad story. A 15-year-old girl was forced to marry a man, but two years later she was murdered for escaping from her husband. Surprisingly, her father ordered her killing. It happened in Asia. I didn't believe this story when I first heard it.

6.3 Discussion: Do you want to get married when you are young? What do you think about child marriage?

7 Reading graphs and charts

Check how the past simple and the past progressive are used and discuss social and gender situations in groups

Data presented here was used in the preparation of the Human Development Report Website. The table shows how the social and gender situations between Afghanistan and Japan were changing from 2000 to 2018.

	Afghanistan		Japan	
Year	2000	2018	2000	2018
Life expectancy at birth (years)	55.8	64.5	81.2	84.5
Expected years of schooling, female (years)	0.6	7.9	14.1	15.2
Expected years of schooling, male (years)	7.5	12.5	14.4	15.3
Adolescent birth rate (births per 1,000 women aged 15-19)	165.2	69.0	4.4	3.8
Estimated gross national income per capita, female (US dollar)	445	1,102	22,743	28,781
Estimated gross national income per capita, male (US dollar)	1,167	2,355	46,452	53,387

http://hdr.undp.org/en/countries Source: Human Development Reports

8 Research

Try to do some research and make a presentation using slides, a poster or a handout

Tips for doing your research

1) Define the term(s), such as gender equality, inequality or gender bias
2) Identify the problems of gender equality and inequality that SDG 5 and SDG 10 show
3) Examine the realities around you with regards to SDG 5 and SDG 10
4) Check the local or global efforts that are being done to achieve SDG 5 and SDG 10
5) Explain what you can do to achieve SDG 5 and SDG 10
6) Refer to the local policies that aim to solve the problems of gender equality and inequality
7) Propose your own ideas or actions to solve these problems

Sample

Girls' education in Afghanistan

United Nations

Afghanistan	HDI: 0.496	World Rank: 170
Japan	HDI: 0.915	World Rank: 19

*HDI (the Human Development Index) = an index that measures key dimensions of human development.

- *Worldwide, 132 million girls are out of school*
- *Gender-equitable education systems help keep both girls and boys in school, building prosperity for entire countries*

Background The Taliban forbid girls' education in Afghanistan

Shabana Basij-Rasikh dressed as a boy and went to a secret school. It was the only way that girls could study.

Shabana Basij-Rasikh ©SOLA

Shabana is now the President of **the School of Leadership, Afghanistan (SOLA)**. SOLA is an Afghanistan-led first private boarding school to provide education opportunities and security for girls.

©SOLA

FACT on girls' education in Afghanistan

- 3.7 million children are out of school and 60 % are girls.
- The level of literacy among boys is much higher at 66 %, while the literacy rate of girl is just 37 %.
- Fewer than one out of five teachers is female.
- 71 % of children out of school in Afghanistan are female.
- Only 32 % of adult females (ages 15-24) are literate.
- One-third of girls under age 18 get married.

Unit 5 Clean Water and Sanitation

安全な水とトイレを世界中に

Goal 6 Ensure access to water and sanitation for all

1 Background (facts & figures)

Which facts and figures are you interested in?

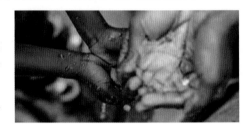

- Now, more than **2 billion people** are living with the risk of reduced access to freshwater resources.

- By 2050, at least **one in four people** is likely to live in a country affected by chronic or recurring **shortages of freshwater**.

2 Topic-related vocabulary check

CD 015
↓ 015

2.1 Listen and fill in the blanks

words	meaning
human waste *n.*	the ( ) that the human body gets rid of when we go to the toilet [＝物]
hygiene *n.*	the practice of keeping your body ( ) in order to prevent illness and disease [＝清潔な]
irrigation *n.*	the process of supplying land with water in order for ( ) and plants to grow on it [＝作物]
diarrhea *n.*	loose and watery stool during a bowel movement, in which your solid waste is more ( ) than usual [＝液状の]
open defecation *n.*	the act of going to the toilet or discharging solid waste ( ) [＝外で]
infrastructure *n.*	the basic, underlying framework of a system and ( ), such as power plants, schools and transportation systems [＝サービス]
mitigation *n.*	the act of ( ) how harmful, serious or unpleasant things are [＝減らす]

2.2 Ask each other in pairs

A: What does "open defection" mean? Please explain it to me.

B: "Open defection" means the act of going to the toilet or discharging solid waste outside.

3 Knowledge check (quiz)

3.1 Look up the answer online

1) How much of the global population suffers from water scarcity?

a) 25 %.   b) 40 %.   c) 60 %.

2) How many people lack access to basic sanitation services in the world?

a) 2.4 billion people.

b) 98 million people.

c) 980,000 people.

3) Around _____ people globally use a source of drinking water that is contaminated by human waste.

a) 2.4 billion   b) 1.8 billion   c) 100 million

4) In 2015, 2.9 billion people in the global population had safe sanitation but 2.3 billion people still lacked basic sanitation. What percentage of the global population had safe sanitation in 2015?

a) 29 %.   b) 49 %.   c) 39 %.

5) Approximately _____ of all available water is used for irrigation in the world.

a) 33 %   b) 15 %   c) 70 %

3.2 Do some research online and discuss the following questions with your classmates

1) Do you think the number of people who suffer from water scarcity will increase or decrease in the next 10 years? Do you think this problem depends on climate change?

e.g. I think the number of people who will suffer from water scarcity is increasing, because there will be more droughts which will affect people's access to water.

2) Why do so many people around the world use a source of water contaminated by human waste?

e.g. I think this is because many people do not have access to basic sanitation facilities and the water is not thoroughly cleaned before consumption.

4.1 Listen and fill in the blanks

Goal 6 Ensure access to water and sanitation for all

- Access to water, sanitation and (¹   ) is a basic human right, yet billions of people still find it difficult to even get the most basic of water services. Around (²   ) billion people globally use a (³   ) of drinking water that is fecally contaminated. This means that it has not been cleaned and treated and is polluted with human waste.

- Contaminated water and bad (⁴   ) can lead to illness and more than (⁵   ) children die every day from diarrheal diseases. (⁶   ) million people remain without even basic drinking water services and 1 out of 4 healthcare facilities (⁷   ) basic drinking water supplies on a worldwide basis. In order to give these millions of people access to basic services and safe drinking water, we (⁸   ) invest in good infrastructure, create sanitation facilities and (⁹   ) people on good hygiene (¹⁰   ).

- Throughout the world there are (¹¹   ) of people who lack basic sanitation. Basic sanitation means people have (¹²   ) that ensure hygienic separation of human waste from human contact. They include having (¹³   ) toilets. Some 2.4 billion people lack access to basic sanitation services. Now, around (¹⁴   ) million people practice open defecation. This means that people go to the toilet outside in the open environment. This is a very serious problem and every 20 (¹⁵   ) a child dies because of poor sanitation.

4.2 Questions for discussion

1) Which goal is the most important to achieve, drinking water or basic sanitation?
2) What do you think about children who suffer from bad sanitation and water supplies?
3) Why do you think millions of people do not have basic water services?
4) What can we do to give people access to basic sanitation and encourage good hygiene?

5.1 Do you know about World Water Day?

World Water Day takes place on the 22nd of March every year. The day helps people understand the importance of water and aims to raise awareness of billions of people who live without access to safe water. The day is also useful to make people familiar with SDG 6: clean water and sanitation for all by 2030.

©UN Water

World Water Day has a different theme every year. The theme in 2020 is on water and climate change. Climate change <u>can</u> influence the quality and supply of our water. Water is becoming even more scarce and polluted through extreme weather events such as flooding and droughts. Flooding <u>can</u> cause huge damage to people's homes, agriculture, hygiene, and infrastructure.

People need water for basic sanitation and healthcare. If strong and durable WASH (water, sanitation and hygiene) facilities are built in poor communities, they <u>could</u> provide people with clean water and the sanitation they need. In addition, these communities will be able to combat longer dry seasons and flooding. WASH services <u>can</u> also help reduce risks of diseases and raise living standards.

As for climate change, experts <u>can</u> predict higher temperatures and more extreme weather conditions. These extreme weather conditions <u>could</u> affect the availability and distribution of rainfall, river flow and groundwater. They <u>could</u> also deteriorate water quality. Poor communities have already been affected by bad water supplies. Climate change <u>will</u> most likely damage them in the future. Water is therefore a key factor to help adapt to climate change.

Clean water and sanitation as stated in SDG 6 have a strong relationship with climate action in SDG 13. It sets out the goal to take urgent action to combat climate change and its impact. Climate change <u>can</u> affect the water cycle, so climate action is very important to achieve SDG 6.

5.2 Discussion points

1) How can natural disasters affect water supplies and sanitation services?
2) What should we do to help poor communities achieve this SDG?
3) Are you trying to save water in your daily life? What are you doing about it.
4) Are you worried about climate change?

Grammar point　auxiliary verbs（助動詞）

文中の下線部 can, could, will などの助動詞は、話し手の気持ちや態度を表し、事実とは異なる主観的な感情を表します。

e.g. Clean water **could** save thousands of lives.

6　Basic grammar exercises: auxiliary verbs

6.1　Choose the appropriate answer

We know that clean water, along with decent sanitation and hygiene, is very effective in reducing poverty. It can help save lives, drive economic growth, keep children in school and increase opportunities for women and girls. If investment is given to help improve water and sanitation services, many child deaths in poor regions [1](may / must) be reduced. Many more children [2](could / must) also go to school if they had adequate drinking water and sanitation facilities. If we are to eradicate diseases, good hygiene [3](must / could) be practiced. If health conditions improve and better water and sanitation facilities are available, workers [4](will / should) increase productivity and people over 60 [5](will / should) live longer.

6.2　Read aloud the text to see how auxiliary verbs are used

Basic clean water and sanitation is a must for everyone in the world. If everyone had basic drinking facilities and adequate sanitation, disease could be reduced and there would be a better chance for everyone to be healthy and live a longer and more comfortable life.

6.3　Discussion: What could happen if water and sanitation services were improved around the world?

7　Reading graphs and charts

Check how auxiliary verbs are used and discuss clean water in groups

We should not waste our water and everyone can help in keeping our water clean. For example, we can participate in river cleanups. We must also avoid flushing things down the toilet that are not biodegradable. They can end up polluting our beaches and water. If we could all do such simple things and know about where our water comes from, we could make sure that future generations also have access to this valuable resource.

https://www.behance.net/gallery/20611539/
Water-Sanitation-and-Hygiene-Infographics

8 Research

Try to do some research and make a presentation using slides, a poster or a handout

Tips for doing your research

1) Define the term(s), such as clean water and sanitation
2) Identify the problems of clean water and sanitation that SDG 6 shows
3) Examine the realities around you with regards to SDG 6
4) Check the local or global efforts that are being done to achieve SDG 6
5) Explain what you can do to achieve SDG 6
6) Refer to the local policies that aim to solve the problems of clean water and sanitation
7) Propose your own ideas or actions to solve these problems

Poster sample

Clean water and climate change

- We need clean water
- Climate change can affect rainfall, river flow and groundwater
- Climate change can deteriorate water quality

 Take action!

- Don't let your water consumption run out of control
- Save water, money and energy
- Don't wash clothes every day
- Get a low-flush toilet
- Cut down on meat and dairy, and eat seasonal vegetables
- Reduce food waste

WASH
(Water, Sanitation and Hygiene)

WASH is essential!

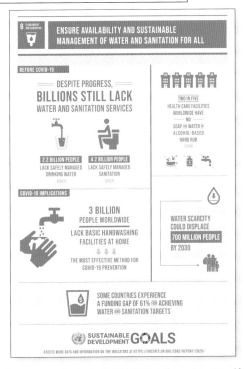

https://www.un.org/sustainabledevelopment/wp-content/uploads/2019/07/E_Infographic_06.pdf

Unit 6 — Affordable and Clean Energy

エネルギーをみんなにそしてクリーンに

Goal 7 Ensure access to affordable, reliable, sustainable and modern energy

---

1 Background (facts & figures)

Which facts and figures are you interested in?

- In 2017, **840 million people** didn't have access to electricity, mostly in sub-Saharan Africa.
- Since 2015, the world has obtained **17.5 % of its total final energy consumption** from renewable sources.

---

2 Topic-related vocabulary check

CD 018
↓ 018

2.1 Listen and fill in the blanks

words	meaning
affordable *adj.*	(　　　　　　) or reasonable enough for most people to afford [= 安価]
renewable *adj.*	capable of being replaced (　　　　　) or easily without the risk of using energy and natural resources [= 自然に]
carbon dioxide *n.*	the (　　　　　) produced when people breathe out, wood is burned in the air, or foods decay [= ガス]
pollute *v.*	to make air, water or soil terribly (　　　　　) and not suitable for us [= 汚れた]
alternative *adj.*	relating to activities that are (　　　　　) from what is usual or traditional [= 異なる]
replenish *v.*	to (　　　　　) something up again [= 満たす]
emission *n.*	the act of sending out gas, (　　　　　), light, etc. [= 熱]
hydroelectricity *n.*	electricity produced by the force of fast-moving (　　　　　) such as rivers or waterfalls [= 水]
geothermal *adj.*	related to using the heat inside the (　　　　　) [= 地球]
biomass *n.*	plant and (　　　　　) matter used to provide power or energy [= 動物]

2.2 Ask each other in pairs

    A： What does "replenish" mean? Please explain it to me.

    B： "Replenish" means to fill something up again.

Knowledge check (quiz)

3.1 Look up the answer online

1) Clean energy cannot be produced with _____.
   a) coal
   b) sun
   c) wind
   d) waves

2) Which gas in the atmosphere causes global warming?
   a) Ozone.
   b) Carbon dioxide.
   c) Mustard gas.

3) How many people cook with open fires or simple stoves fueled by kerosene, biomass and coal?
   a) Approximatelly 1 million.
   b) Approximatelly 20 million.
   c) Approximatelly 3 billion.

4) Where do 87 % of people live without electricity?
   a) Urban areas.   b) Rural areas.

5) Which country has introduced wind-powered electricity the most?
   a) China.
   b) The U.S.
   c) Germany.

3.2 Do some research online and discuss the following questions with your classmates

1) What can we do to save electricity? Is there anything you can do now?
   e.g. I think unplugging appliances is something I can easily do. I can also use my bike or public transport to go to school. This will reduce carbon emissions.

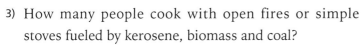

2) Why has renewable energy made little progress in Japan?
   e.g. I looked into renewable energy. I found out that there are three main obstacles in Japan. These are, technical problems, economic problems and social problems.

4.1 Listen and fill in the blanks

CD 019
↓ 019

Goal 7 Ensure access to affordable, reliable, sustainable and modern energy

- About 800 million people live without electricity and approximately 3 billion people lack (¹   ) to clean-cooking solutions. Those people burn carbon (²   ) for cooking and heating, and they (³   ) large amounts of greenhouse gases. They not only cause (⁴   ) but also have harmful impacts on people's health and the environment such as air (⁵   ).
- Lack of electricity affects people's health, their (⁶   ) opportunities and their livelihoods. Without electricity, medical (⁷   ) in hospitals cannot be (⁸   ), many school children cannot finish their homework, people cannot work at night, and refrigerators cannot safely (⁹   ) food, medicine and vaccine.
- In order to (¹⁰   ) the electricity problem, it is necessary to find clean, efficient, and (¹¹   ) energy sources. Renewable energy sources are thought to be the best (¹²   ) to fossil fuels. They are constantly replenished through natural (¹³   ), and have a very limited (¹⁴   ) impact on the environment.
- There are five main (¹⁵   ) considered renewable energy sources. One of the most popular renewable energy sources is solar power. It comes from the sun. Wind power is generated from wind spinning massive turbines. Hydroelectricity is produced by moving water at dams or (¹⁶   ). Geothermal energy comes from the earth's (¹⁷   ) heat. Biomass, such as agricultural crops, food, wood waste, animal manure and human sewage, is burned or (¹⁸   ) into gas to produce heat.

4.2 Questions for discussion
1) What are the problems of having no access to clean-cooking?
2) If we don't have electricity, what kind of problems do we have?
3) What do you think about renewable energy sources?
4) Do you know any technologies that are considered renewable energy sources?

5.1 Do you know about the pellet stove? Have you ever heard about carbon neutral?

A pellet stove is a heating appliance that works by burning wood pellets as fuel. Although pellet stoves have similar principles as wood stoves that burn firewood, they are considered to be more <u>environmentally</u> <u>friendly</u>. Why? Wood pellets are produced by crushing and densifying waste timber like sawdust, forestry residues, and industrial by-products. They would otherwise be dumped into landfills or left in the forest.

Since wood pellets are made from trees that absorb carbon dioxide, they are carbon neutral biomass energy. Growing trees captures carbon dioxide emitted by wood pellet combustion. Moreover, the level of carbon dioxide released by burning wood pellets is similar to the level of carbon dioxide exhausted when wood is decomposed <u>naturally</u> on the forest floor. In this way, unlike fossil fuels which only release carbon dioxide in a unilateral way, wood pellets are considered carbon neutral.

Pellet stoves have many advantages. They produce lower ash content of about 0.5 to 1 %, and emit very low toxic chemicals and smoke, compared to fossil fuel stoves. Pellet stoves are also easy to use and <u>highly</u> efficient, since they contain an automatic ignition and a power modulation. Wood pellets are affordable and less expensive than fossil fuels and electricity. Moreover, pellet stoves are very easy to install.

However, pellet stoves also have some disadvantages. The burn pot of the stove needs to be cleaned every week. It also needs to be checked by a professional every year. Moreover, it may cost around 2,000 dollars or more depending on the model. Would you like to install a pellet stove in your house?

5.2 Discussion points

1) What do you think about pellet stoves? Do you think they are a good idea?
2) Is it true that wood pellets are renewable but carbon neutral?
3) Do you understand the advantages and disadvantages of wood pellets and pellet stoves?
4) What can we do to expand the use of renewable energy?

Grammar point　adjectives and adverbs（形容詞・副詞）

文中の下線部 environmentally, naturally, highly は副詞で、それぞれ形容詞（friendly）、動詞（decomposed）、形容詞（efficient）を修飾しています。形容詞は名詞を修飾し補語としても働きます。（➡文法マスター参照）

e.g. Wood pellets are **quite readily available**.

6　Basic grammar exercises: adjectives and adverbs

6.1　Choose the appropriate answer

1) People in sub-Saharan Africa don't have (reliability / reliable) access to electricity.
2) The share of renewable energy is (rapid / rapidly) increasing in the world.
3) The amount of wind power energy in China is the (highest / highly) in the world.
4) We need to use electricity (wise / wisely) and efficiently.

6.2　Read aloud the text and see how adverbs and adjectives are used

A feed-in tariff is an economic policy which is created to promote active investment in renewable energy sources. Since anyone who produces renewable energy can sell the electricity to an electric power company at quite high fixed prices for a long term, it seems a pretty good deal. However, after the contract has expired, we actually won't be able to sell it at a reasonable price. I think this is a serious problem.

6.3　Discussion: Do you agree with the idea of the feed-in tariff?

7　Reading graphs and charts

Check how adjectives and adverbs are used and discuss energy in groups

Look at the two graphs on the right. In 2013, LNG accounted for 43.2 % of Japan's power generation, and coal and oil accounted for 30.3 % and 14.9 % respectively. Nuclear power accounted for just 1.7 %. In 2015 however, a proposal for Japan to increase nuclear power from 20 to 22 % by 2030 was introduced. The plan scaled back fossil fuel use and also called for an expansion of renewable energy sources.

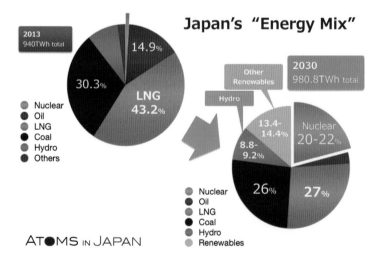

8 | Research

Try to do some research and make a presentation using slides, a poster or handout

Tips for doing your research

1) Define the term(s), such as carbon neutral and renewable energy
2) Identify the problems of energy that SDG 7 shows
3) Examine the realities around you with regards to SDG 7
4) Check the local or global efforts that are being done to achieve SDG 7
5) Explain what you can do to achieve SDG 7
6) Refer to the local government policies to solve the problems of energy
7) Propose your own ideas or actions to solve these problems

Sample

Renewable energy

CLIL University
Sanshu Taro

1

Question!

Have you ever heard about biomass energy?

2

Realities and Problems

- Realities
  We rely on fossil fuels 85.5% of the time.
  We only use renewable energy about 10% of the time.
- Problems
  We only have a limited amount of fossil fuels.
  Burning fossil fuels release green house gases.
  The global population is increasing.

3

What can we do?

Renewable energy (clean energy) will be the solution!

✓Solar power
✓Wind power
✓Hydroelectric power
✓Biomass energy
✓Geothermal energy

4

World Energy consumption

Neutral Gas 3082 Mtoe 23.40 %
Nuclear 2577 TWh 4.43 %
Hydroelectric 3946 TWh 6.78 %
Wind 841 TWh 1.45 %
Solar 253.0 TWh 0.43 %
Biofuel 75 TWh 0.57 %
Other 518 TWh 0.89 %
Coal 3840 Mtoe 29.06 %
Petroleum 4331 Mtoe 32.89 %
World Energy Consumption by Fuel (2015)
Fossil Fuel 85.5 % Renewable 10.1 %

5

Biomass energy

- Biomass is renewable energy from plants and animals, and it also contains energy from the sun.
- Examples of biomass
➤Wood
➤Garbage
➤Crops
➤Landfill gas
➤Alcohol fuels

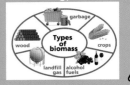

6

Unit 7

Decent Work and Economic Growth

働きがいも経済成長も

Goal 8 Promote sustained, inclusive and sustainable economic growth, full and productive employment and decent work for all

1 Background (facts & figures)

Which facts and figures are you interested in?

- **One fifth of young people** are not in education, employment or training.
- Around the world, **218 million children aged 5 to 17** are in employment. Among them, **152 million children** are trapped in child labor.

©ACE

2 Topic-related vocabulary check

CD 021
↓ 021

2.1 Listen and fill in the blanks

words	meaning
decent *adj.*	of an adequate good enough standard or (　　　　　) [= 質]
employ *v.*	to give (　　　　　) to people and pay them for it [= 仕事]
unemployment *n.*	a (　　　　　) in which some people don't have work [= 状況]
significant *adj.*	having an important (　　　　　) on what will happen in the future [= 影響]
child labor *n.*	the use of children who are legally too (　　　　　) to work [= 若い]
force *v.*	to make (　　　　　) do things they don't want to do [= 人々]
earnings *n.*	the amount of (　　　　　) paid for the work [= お金]
afford *v.*	to have (　　　　　) money or time to buy or do something [= 十分な]
opportunity *n.*	a (　　　　　) or occasion that makes it possible to do something [= 機会]
vocational *adj.*	relating to education and skills you need to do a (　　　　　) job [= 特定の]
engage in *v.*	to become involved in an (　　　　　) [= 活動]

2.2 Ask each other in pairs

A: What does "child labor" mean? Please explain it to me.

B: "Child labor" means the use of children who are legally too young to work.

44

3 Knowledge check (quiz)

3.1 Look up the answer online

1) What proportion of young people in the world are not engaged in education, employment or training?

    a) 30 %.   b) 20 %.   c) 10 %.

2) Is it true that women earn less than men around the world?

    a) Yes, it is. The global gender pay gap stands at 23 %.

    b) No, it isn't. There is no gender pay gap around the world.

©ACE

3) The adults unemployment rate was 4 %, but the youth unemployment rate was _____ in 2018.

    a) 2 %   b) 12 %   c) 22 %

4) How many children are engaged in child labor?

    a) 73 million.

    b) 152 million.

    c) 218 million.

©ACE

5) Which of the following can force children into child labor the most in Ghana?

    a) Cotton.

    b) Cocoa.

    c) Banana.

3.2 Do some research online and discuss the following questions with your classmates

1) Do you think there is a relationship between education and decent work ?

    e.g. Yes. I did research on education and decent work. I found out that young people in poor countries have no schooling.

©ACE

2) Do you agree with child labor? Why does child labor occur in some countries?

    e.g. No, of course not. I don't agree with child labor. However, there are some reasons for it. I think people are very poor and couldn't live if children didn't work.

4 Understanding SDGs | Decent work and economic growth

4.1 Listen and fill in the blanks

Goal 8 Promote sustained, inclusive and sustainable economic growth, full and productive employment and decent work for all

- Since the global economic downturn of 2009, labor productivity has been (^{1}) in the world. In 2018, labor productivity increased by (^{2}) percent globally and it was the highest annual growth since 2010. However, significant differences are found across (^{3}). Between 2017 and 2018, labor productivity grew the most in Asia, while (^{4}) changed in sub-Saharan Africa and Latin America.

- We need to reduce the (^{5}) pay gap. Women still earn (^{6}) than men. Based on some data, men's hourly pay is (^{7}) percent higher than that of women. Gender pay gaps are (^{8}) in social norms and cultural expectations about women's roles in society.

- We further need to increase employment opportunities, particularly for young people. In 2018, youths were (^{9}) times more likely to be (^{10}) than adults, and one (^{11}) of young people are not (^{12}) in either education, employment or training. These young people are labeled NEET (Not in Education, Employment, or Training). In other words, they were neither gaining professional experience nor developing skills through educational or (^{13}) programs in their prime years. Young women were also more than (^{14}) as likely as young men to be unemployed, outside the labor force, and not in school or in a training program.

- We have to eradicate (^{15}) labor and end child labor in all its forms. Around the world, more than (^{16}) million children are engaged in child labor, and (^{17}) of them are in hazardous work. Child labor endangers children's health, safety, and moral (^{18}).

4.2 Questions for discussion
1) Which target are you interested in, decent work or economic growth?
2) Do you think the working environment in your country is safe and secure?
3) Do you think the number of young people labelled NEET is decreasing now?
4) What can you do to reduce inequalities across age groups and genders?

5 Reading | Child labor

5.1 Do you know where chocolate comes from?

In 2016, 152 million children around the world remained <u>trapped</u> in child labor. Today, a lot of children in Ghana are still forced to work in cocoa farms under life <u>threatening</u> conditions, such as using sharp tools, spraying pesticides, carrying heavy things or working long hours in the sun. Those children are not allowed to go to school. The main reason why they have to work is poverty. Most cocoa farms are on such a small scale that farmers cannot make a living by only producing cacao beans. They can't afford to send their children to school. More severely, some children are victims of human trafficking in poorer areas.

In 2009, ACE, which is a Japanese NGO, launched "SMILE-Ghana Project" to protect children from child labor and support their education in partnership with the local NGO. ACE monitors where child labor exists, improves school environments, and establishes child committees where children can talk about their own problems and convey their opinions to adults. ACE also provides cocoa farmers with training in agricultural techniques to enhance productivity and earnings.

<u>Mobilizing</u> local resources and <u>improving</u> the livelihood of the community, the project has removed more than 450 children from child labor and enrolled them into schools. It has helped more than 6,000 children by improving school environments. In 2016, ACE succeeded in making child labor-free chocolate <u>produced</u> by the project. Next time you see chocolate, think about where it comes from and whether or not it is child labor-free.

©ACE
http://acejapan.org/choco/smile-ghana

5.2 Discussion points

1) Why are a lot of children in Ghana forced to work?
2) What are examples of ACE's activities?
3) What do you think about chocolate produced by child labor?
4) Do you know any other goods produced by child labor?

Grammar point　participles（分詞）

文中の下線部 trapped, threatening, mobilizing, improving, produced は分詞です。現在分詞（動詞の -ing 形）と過去分詞（動詞の -ed 形）があり、形容詞の働きをしたり、分詞構文として使われます。（➡文法マスター参照）

e.g. a **developing** country（開発途上国）　a **developed** country（先進国）

6　Basic grammar exercises: participles

6.1　Choose the appropriate answer

1) An (estimated / estimating) 172 million people were without work in 2018.

2) There are few people (engaged / engaging) in education, employment or training.

3) To reduce the number of people (lived / living) below the poverty line, we have to create decent, (well-paid / well-paying) jobs.

6.2　Read aloud the text and see how the participle is used

152 million children around the world remain trapped in child labor. Today, a lot of children living in Ghana are still forced to work in cocoa farms under dangerous conditions. Some of them have to work in unpaid situations.

6.3　Discussion: What should both developed and developing countries do to promote safe and secure working environments for all workers?

7　Reading graphs and charts

Check how the participle is used and discuss child labor in groups

The list has a total of 139 goods produced by child labor and forced labor in violation of international standards in 75 countries around the world. There is a total of 379 line items including sugarcane, cotton, bricks, and gold.

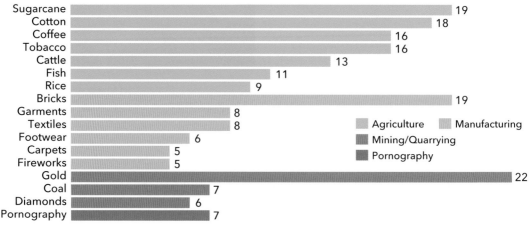

Goods with Most Child Labor and Forced Labor Listings by Number of Countries and Production Sector

- Sugarcane 19
- Cotton 18
- Coffee 16
- Tobacco 16
- Cattle 13
- Fish 11
- Rice 9
- Bricks 19
- Garments 8
- Textiles 8
- Footwear 6
- Carpets 5
- Fireworks 5
- Gold 22
- Coal 7
- Diamonds 6
- Pornography 7

Legend: Agriculture　Manufacturing　Mining/Quarrying　Pornography

https://www.dol.gov/sites/dolgov/files/ILAB/reports/TVPRA_Report2016.pdf

8 Research

Try to do some research and make a presentation using slides, a poster or a handout

Tips for doing your research

1) Define the term(s), such as child labor and hazardous work
2) Identify the problems of child labor or hazardous work that SDG 8 show
3) Examine the realities around you with regards to SDG 8
4) Check the local or global efforts that are being done to achieve SDG 8
5) Show what you can do to achieve SDG 8
6) Refer to the local policies that aim to solve the child labor or hazardous work
7) Propose your own ideas or actions to solve these problems

Sample

End Child Labour

CLIL University
Sanshu Taro

1

How many children are engaged in child labour worldwide?

2

3

About 1 in 10 children are victims of child labour

4

121 million children would still be engaged in child labour in 2025

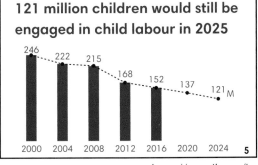

5

71 % work in the agricultural sector

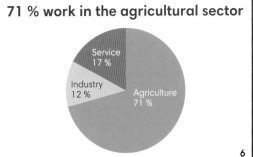

6

https://www.ilo.org/ipec/Informationresources/WCMS_653987/lang--en/index.htm

Unit 8 Industry, Innovation and Infrastructure

産業と技術革新の基盤をつくろう

Goal 9 Build resilient infrastructure, promote inclusive and sustainable industrialization and foster innovation

1 Background (facts & figures)

Which facts and figures are you interested in?

- Global investment in research and development was **$2 trillion in 2016, up from $739 billion in 2000**.
- In 2018, **90 %** of people lived within range of a **3G or higher quality mobile network**, but not all can afford to use it.

2 Topic-related vocabulary check

CD 2-1 ↓ 024

2.1 Listen and fill in the blanks

words	meaning
innovation *n.*	introduction of new (　　　　　) or methods [= 考え]
infrastructure *n.*	basic systems and structures that a (　　　　　) needs to work properly, such as roads, railways, and banks [= 地域社会]
manufacture *n.*	the making of goods or materials, usually in large numbers or amount, often using (　　　　　) [= 機械]
investment *n.*	use of money, or the money used, to get a (　　　　　) or to make a business activity successful [= 利益]
research and development *n.*	part of activities concerned with studying new ideas and (　　　　　) new products [= 計画する]
microcredit *n.*	small amounts of money that are lent to people in poor countries to help them start or maintain a small (　　　　　) [= 事業]
exploit *v.*	to treat people (　　　　　) by asking them to do things, but giving them very little in return [= 不公平に]

2.2 Ask each other in pairs

A: What does "innovation" mean? Please explain it to me.

B: "Innovation" means the introduction of new ideas or methods.

3 Knowledge check (quiz)

3.1 Look up the answer online

1) The gap in industrial productivity between developed and developing countries remains big. In 2018, for instance, manufacturing value added (MVA) per capita was only _____ dollars in the least developed countries (LDCs), compared to 4,938 dollars in Europe and Northern America.

   a) 114   b) 1,114   c) 2,114

2) One of the biggest challenges industries in the LDCs face is lack of access to _____ for everyday business activities.

   a) loans or lines of credit

   b) temporary staff dispatching services

   c) foreign language education

3) In 2016, over 47 % of total MVA came from _____ sectors in East and Southeast Asia, Europe and Northern America. In contrast, the shares in Oceania (excluding Australia and New Zealand) and sub-Saharan Africa were only 1.9 % and 14.9 % respectively.

   a) traditional handicrafts   b) heavy metal   c) medium-high and high-tech

4) In 2016, 2.21 % of GDP was spent on _____ in Europe and Northern America, compared to 0.42 % in sub-Saharan Africa and 0.83 % in Western Asia.

   a) mining

   b) public transportation development

   c) research and development

5) More than half of the world's population is currently using _____, but the rates are much lower in the LDCs (about 20 %).

   a) cellular phones   b) the Internet   c) electric cars

3.2 Do some research online and discuss the following questions with your classmates

1) Which countries are called the LDCs? Are there any differences between developing countries and the LDCs?

   e.g. I think Benin, Mali and Togo are called the LDCs, but I don't know there are many differences between developing countries and the LDCs.

2) How would your life be without the Internet?

   e.g. We wouldn't be able to get enough information about global issues.

4.1 Listen and fill in the blanks

Goal 9 Build resilient infrastructure, promote inclusive and sustainable industrialization and foster innovation

- Inclusive and sustainable industrialization is a key to developing countries' economic (¹   ) and social development. Developed countries have established highly industrialized societies based on (²   ) in infrastructure, industrial development and technological progress.

- As has often been the case in developed countries, industrial development may (³   ) some serious problems. First, it may cause environmental problems such as air or water (⁴   ) and deforestation, which can lead to instability and destruction of people's lives, bad health conditions of the residents in the polluted areas, and loss of (⁵   ). It may also cause social disparity, in which poor workers may be (⁶   ) by only a few successful people. To prevent these problems from happening, we need to realize inclusive and (⁷   ) industrialization in all areas of the world.

- Basic (⁸   ), such as roads, electricity, water and sanitation, supports our lives. In many developing countries, however, it remains scarce. 3 in 10 people in the world do not have (⁹   ) to safe drinking water, and about 40 % of people worldwide lack access to basic (¹⁰   ).

- Research and development, or R&D, plays a key role in industrial development and (¹¹   ). Many developing countries, however, can't afford to advance further due to lack of enough budget, facilities, and human (¹²   ).

4.2 Questions for discussion

1) Do you think all developing countries should be industrialized like developed countries? Why or why not?

2) What does "inclusive and sustainable industrialization" mean?

3) What should developing countries do to advance R&D (research and development)?

5.1 How to improve small-scale businesses in developing countries

It is not easy for small-scale industry workers in developing countries to open a savings account and receive loans. That is because banks regard their financial status as unstable and do not trust them as good customers. In order to encourage them to save money or receive loans, <u>some groups or organizations are</u> making efforts.

The first example of such organizations is Grameen Bank in Bangladesh. Established in 1983, the Grameen Bank has been encouraging the poor, especially women, to start or develop their business. It offers collateral free low interest loans. Customers are told to apply for the loan in small groups. <u>The bank gives</u> them a small amount of loan, called microcredit, to the group. Then the groups are asked to repay it with fixed interest within a certain period of time. According to the bank, <u>the number of borrowers</u> <u>reached</u> 9 million in 2018, and now it has various programs for the development of education, agriculture, and information technology in Bangladesh.

Another example is the activities implemented by FINCA Peru, which is a non-governmental microfinace organization operating in Peru. Not only does it offer microcredit to local women who run small businesses, but also gives business workshops on bookkeeping, understanding seasonal trends, how to stock goods, and so on. Research shows that the group of women who participated in the workshop attained significantly higher profit than those who didn't.

These are only some of the examples that are working very well to encourage poor people to run their businesses successfully. We must keep searching for better ways that are suitable for each situation.

5.2 Discussion points

1) What are the bank's criteria to give a loan to a customer?
2) Have you ever heard of the word "microcredit"?
3) Do you think microcredit is a good way to help poor women make their financial status better? Why or why not?
4) Besides giving loans and giving business workshops, what is a good way for poor women to break free from poverty in developing countries?

Grammar point　subjects and verbs（主語と動詞の一致）

文中の下線部 some groups or organizations are ..., The Bank gives ..., the number of borrowers reached ... の例のように、主語と動詞は人称や時制を一致させる原則があります。（➡文法マスター参照）

　　　e.g. **Everyone** in this village **works** as a farmer.

6　Basic grammar exercises: subjects and verbs

6.1　Choose the appropriate answer

1) Over half of the population in the world (is / are) using the Internet.

2) In some countries the police (don't check / doesn't check) the rate of interest, and money lenders (impose / imposes) a very high rate of interest on borrowers.

3) The school (have / has) five classrooms, but each of them (have / has) only four desks and chairs.

4) In Europe and Northern America, 2.21 % of GDP (was / were) spent on research and development in 2016.

6.2　Read aloud the text and see how subjects and verbs are used

Many LDCs depend on imports from other countries in terms of medium-high and high-tech products. They need to develop more researchers and experts in the field to improve their domestic manufacturing, but not all countries have good education systems to realize it. Every country needs to establish and implement a good education system first in order to develop domestic industries.

6.3　Discussion: What is the best way to develop experts in high-tech industry?

7　Reading graphs and charts

Check how subjects and verbs are used and discuss manufacturing in groups

The manufacturing sectors are less and less important for national incomes of both developing and developed countries. The share of manufacturing value added (MVA) accounted for a quarter or more in most countries in 1980s, but it has been declining globally. As a result, there are fewer manufacturing workers in many countries. About 7.5 million jobs have been lost since 1980. These job losses have likely contributed to the declining labor force participation rate of recent years.

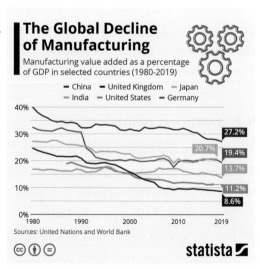

The Global Decline of Manufacturing

Manufacturing value added as a percentage of GDP in selected countries (1980-2019)

- China　- United Kingdom　- Japan
- India　- United States　- Germany

27.2%
20.7%
19.4%
13.7%
11.2%
8.6%

Sources: United Nations and World Bank

statista

Try to do some research and make a presentation using slides, a poster or a handout

Tips for doing your research

1) Define the term(s), such as innovation, infrastructure, and R&D
2) Identify the problems of industry, innovation and infrastructure that SDG 9 shows
3) Examine the realities around you with regards to SDG 9
4) Check the local or global efforts that are being done to achieve SDG 9
5) Explain what you can do to achieve SDG 9
6) Refer to the local policies that aim to solve the problems of industry, innovation and infrastructure
7) Propose your own ideas or actions to solve these problems

Sample

Importance of ICT in the LDCs

Comparing Internet Access
in Japan and Burkina Faso

Sanshu Hana
CLIL University

1

Burkina Faso (BF)

- Land area: 274,000 km² (about 70 % of Japan's land area)
- Population: 19,193,000 (as of 2017)
- Capital: Ouagadougou
- Languages:
  French (official), native African languages belonging Sudanic family
- Muslim (61.5 %), Roman Catholic (23.3 %)

2

Industry and ICT

- Communication (domestic / international)
- Research and development
- Education

3

Data comparison

(as of 2017)	Japan	Burkina Faso
Population	126,786,000	19,193,000
Nominal GDP per capital (US$)	38,313 [25]	644 [180]
Number of Internet users	115,849,200	3,047,000
Ratio of Internet users (%)	90.97 [25]	15.88* [182]

[ ]: international rank * Estimated 4

Hypothesis

- GDP and Internet diffusion: highly correlated

⬇

- Rising Internet diffusion may help develop industry of the country

5

How to help BF develop its ICT

- Human resources
- Education (system / teacher development)
- Exchange program (universities / companies)

6

Unit 9 — Sustainable Cities and Communities

住み続けられるまちづくりを

Goal 11 Make cities and human settlements inclusive, safe, resilient and sustainable

1 Background (facts & figures)

Which facts and figures are you interested in?

- **More than half of humanity – 4.2 billion people** – live in cities today and 6.5 billion people are projected to live in cities by 2050.
- **One out of 4 urban residents** live in slum-like conditions.

2 Topic-related vocabulary check

CD 2-4
027

2.1 Listen and fill in the blanks

words	meaning
urban *adj.*	situated in or relating to a town or (　　　　　) [= 都市]
slum *n.*	a poor and crowded area where people live in (　　　　　) conditions [= 悪い]
waste collection *n.*	the (　　　　　) and transport of waste and unwanted materials [= 収集]
disposal *n.*	a device to reduce (　　　　　) [= ゴミ]
public transport *n.*	a system of vehicles such as (　　　　　) and trains, that are available for everyone [= バス]
resilience *n.*	the ability to become strong, happy, or successful again after a (　　　　　) situation or event [= 困難な]
vulnerable *adj.*	capable of being (　　　　　), mentally or emotionally hurt [= 肉体的に]
exacerbate *v.*	to make a bad situation (　　　　　) [= より悪い]
jeopardize *v.*	to put someone or something in (　　　　　) [= 危険]
hand-to-mouth *adj.*	having just enough (　　　　　) and food to live [= お金]

2.2 Ask each other in pairs

A: What does "slum" mean? Please explain it to me.

B: "Slum" means a poor and crowded area where people live in a very bad conditions.

3 Knowledge check (quiz)

3.1 Look up the answer online

1) Where will 95 percent of urban expansion in the next decade take place?
   a) Developing countries.
   b) Advanced countries.

©Yukiko Abe

2) The world's cities occupy just _____ % of the Earth's land, but account for 60 to 80 % of energy consumption and at least 70 % of carbon emissions.
   a) 3   b) 20   c) 40

3) In 2016, _____ in 10 people living in urban areas breathed polluted air that did not meet the World Health Organization (WHO)'s air quality guidelines value.
   a) 3   b) 5   c) 9

4) What percentage of urban residents have convenient access to public transportation?
   a) Around 50 %.
   b) Around 30 %.
   c) Around 80 %.

5) The _____ Framework for Disaster Risk Reduction 2015-2030 is a global agreement to reduce and prevent disaster risks across the globe.
   a) Sendai   b) Tokyo   c) Hong Kong

©Yukiko Abe

3.2 Do some research online and discuss the following questions with your classmates

1) What kind of benefits do you expect if we have convenient access to public transport?
   e.g. Public transport can reduce air pollution and climate change instead of using cars. In addition, it helps our economic activities and quality of life.

2) What kind of things can you do to reduce the risk of disaster in the world?
   e.g. In my opinion, there is a link between the risk of disaster, poverty, and development. Developing countries are more vulnerable compared to advanced countries.

4.1 Listen and fill in the blanks

Goal 11 Make cities and human settlements inclusive, safe, resilient and sustainable

- Cities face massive (¹   ), socio-economic and spatial challenges. Although they can be a hub for (²   ) development, cities can also exacerbate (³   ). Today many urban residents lack water, sanitation, energy and public (⁴   ). With no land security, many cannot access (⁵   ), adequate homes, jobs, schools and (⁶   ).

- UN-Habitat, the United Nations Programme for Human Settlements, was mandated to address issues of (⁷   ) growth. UN-Habitat supports countries to (⁸   ) living conditions for all through knowledge, policy advice, technical assistance and collaborative action to leave no one and no place behind.

- UN-Habitat has carried out (⁹   ) action in poor and densely populated areas to protect people against COVID-19. In March 2020, the United Nations said, "The impacts of the new coronavirus (¹⁰   ) could be considerably higher on the urban (¹¹   ) living in slums, where overcrowding also makes it (¹²   ) to follow other recommended measures such as social (¹³   ) and self-isolation."

- UN-Habitat is (¹⁴   ) in Nairobi, Kenya. Due to COVID-19 in 2020, many people there had to live hand-to-mouth and it was hard for them to find (¹⁵   ) access points. In addition, they couldn't easily go to those water access points to get water, because they had movement restrictions to prevent further spread of the virus. One local resident said, "We don't have enough water to (¹⁶   ) and (¹⁷   ) our food, so where will we get water to wash our (¹⁸   ) frequently?"

Source: Water access critical to beating back COVID-19 spread in slum areas | UN News / UN-Habitat

4.2 Questions for discussion

1) Do you live in an urban area or a rural area? Please explain your advantages and disadvantages.
2) If you did not have public transport, how would you go to school?
3) Are you still afraid of COVID-19? How do you feel about it?
4) Why are people in slums vulnerable?

5.1 Waste can jeopardize people's life, health and work. Do you think the waste management project in the Maldives is good?

The Maldives, <u>which</u> is proud of its white sand beaches and coral reefs, has trouble in managing solid waste and associated environmental, economic and social issues. Waste jeopardizes the country's major industry, tourism and fishing as well as local people's life and health.

In the Maldives, more than 500,000 people live in the small island nation in the Indian Ocean. Nearly one half of its population lives in Male. The country faces a number of challenges, such as insufficient infrastructure, difficulties with waste transportation and limited budget. Waste management has especially been a critical issue. For example, plastic bottles and bins are overflowing on their beautiful beaches.

Shoko Noda, <u>who</u> has been working for the UN, was one of the key people to contribute to a waste management project. She worked as the head of the UN in the Maldives from 2014 to 2019. The project set strategies to create awareness about waste management and the risk <u>that</u> poor waste management could cause. It established a disposal facility in eleven islands and waste collection systems <u>which</u> local people could manage by themselves. The residents in each island were provided with color-coded trash bins to separate waste at the household level.

Noda said, "More countries can learn a lot from the waste management system in Japan. I hope to see more countries adopt the 3R (reduce, reuse, and recycle), so we can preserve the earth's beautiful nature for future generations."

5.2 Discussion points

1) Why is waste management important?
2) What kind of social issues related to waste did people in the Maldives have?
3) How is the waste management system in your community?
4) What can you do to reduce, reuse and recycle waste?

Grammar point   relative pronouns（関係代名詞）

文中の下線部 which, who, that は関係代名詞です。先行する名詞句などを修飾し補足説明する働きがあります。
（➡文法マスター参照）

e.g. Slums **that** have limited access to water are more vulnerable to COVID-19.

---

6 Basic grammar exercises: relative pronouns

6.1 Choose the appropriate answer

1) Waste is something (that / who) we cannot neglect.

2) Fertilizers, (who / which) are produced from food waste, are vital for plant growth.

3) The Maldives has about 1,200 islands, in (which / that) approximately 200 islands are inhabited.

4) Those (who / which) have easy access to public transport remain low in the Maldives.

5) There are strategies (that / who) can help solve urbanization challenges.

6.2 Read aloud the text and see how the relative pronoun is used

The number of people who live in slums or informal settlements is over 1 billion in the world. There are an estimated 3 billion people that will require adequate and affordable housing by 2030. However, urbanization and population growth are outpacing the construction of new affordable homes.

---

7 Reading graphs and charts

Check how the relative pronoun is used and discuss public transportation in group

Public transport is an essential service for people who live in the city. It is also a catalyst for economic growth and social inclusion which can support their life. There are an increasing number of people who move to urban areas. See the 2018 data from 227 cities in 78 countries. Only 53 % of urban residents had convenient access to public transport.

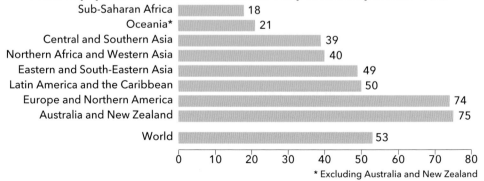

Share of population with convenient access to public transport, 2018 (%)

Sub-Saharan Africa	18
Oceania*	21
Central and Southern Asia	39
Northern Africa and Western Asia	40
Eastern and South-Eastern Asia	49
Latin America and the Caribbean	50
Europe and Northern America	74
Australia and New Zealand	75
World	53

* Excluding Australia and New Zealand

https://unstats.un.org/sdgs/report/2019/The-Sustainable-Development-Goals-Report-2019.pdf

8 Research

Try to do some research and make a presentation using slides, a poster or handout

Tips for doing your research

1) Define the term(s), such as sustainable city and community
2) Identify the problems of sustainable cities and communities that SDG 11 shows
3) Examine the realities around you with regards to SDG 11
4) Check the local or global efforts that are being done to achieve SDG 11
5) Explain what you can do to achieve SDG 11
6) Refer to the local policies that aim to solve the problems of sustainable cities and communities
7) Propose your own ideas or actions to solve these problems

Sample

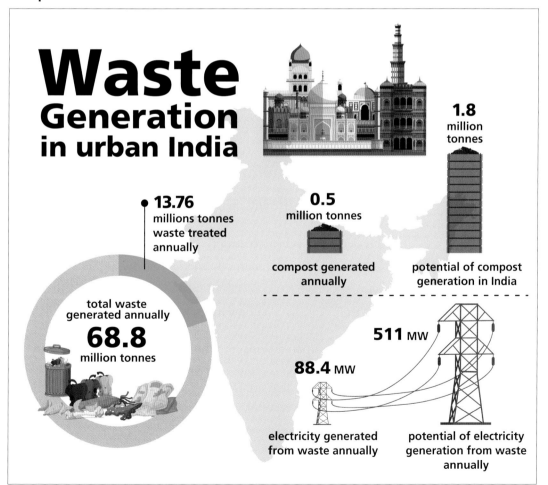

Waste
Generation in urban India

1.8 million tonnes

13.76 millions tonnes waste treated annually

0.5 million tonnes
compost generated annually

potential of compost generation in India

total waste generated annually
68.8 million tonnes

511 MW

88.4 MW

electricity generated from waste annually

potential of electricity generation from waste annually

Unit 10 Responsible Consumption and Production

つくる責任、つかう責任

Goal 12 Ensure sustainable consumption and production patterns

1 Background (facts & figures)

Which facts and figures are you interested in?

- **1.3 billion tons** of food is wasted every year.
- If the global population reaches **9.6 billion by 2050**, we would need nearly **three planets** to provide the natural resources to sustain our current lifestyles.

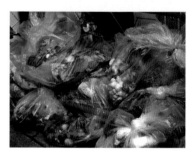

2 Topic-related vocabulary check

CD 2-7
↓ 030

2.1 Listen and fill in the blanks

words	meaning
undernourished *n.*	the state of not eating enough food or getting enough (　　　　　) [= 栄養]
energy efficient *adj.*	using less energy or (　　　　　　) energy consumption [= 減らす]
litter *n.*	small pieces of (　　　　　) that have been left outside [= ごみ]
disposal *n.*	a product that we use and then (　　　　) (　　　　) [= 捨てる]
decompose *v.*	to break down a substance into (　　　　　) parts [= 小さい]
biodegradable *adj.*	able to (　　　　) naturally and harmlessly [= 腐敗する]
landfill *n.*	a place where we (　　　　　) waste material [= 埋める]
ecological footprint *n.*	a way to (　　　　) how much nature we have and use [= 測る]
CO₂ emission *n.*	sending out carbon dioxide into the atmosphere, stemming from the burning of (　　　　) (　　　　) [= 化石燃料]
livestock *n.*	animals and birds that are raised and kept on a (　　　　　) [= 牧場]

2.2 Ask each other in pairs

A: What does "livestock" mean? Please explain it to me.

B: "Livestock" means animals and birds that are raised and kept on a farm.

62

3 Knowledge check (quiz)

3.1 Look up the answer online

1) If everyone used energy efficient lightbulbs, how
   much money would be saved a year?
   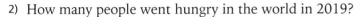
   a) 120 thousand dollars.
   b) 120 billion dollars.
   c) 120 million dollars.

2) How many people went hungry in the world in 2019?
   a) 590 million people.
   b) 690 million people.
   c) 790 million people.

3) All the households in the world use 29 % of global energy. This
   means that such usage contributes to _____ of CO_2 emissions.
   a) 21 %   b) 49 %   c) 77 %

4) In the 1950's the global consumption of plastic materials was around 5 million
   tons, and today it is nearly _____ .
   a) 3.8 billion   b) 380 million   c) 3.8 trillion

5) 130 gallons of water is needed to make half a kilo of
   wheat. In order to produce certain kinds of meat, the
   amount of water used can be multiplied _____ .
   a) 1,000 times   b) 100 times   c) 5 to 10 times

3.2 Do some research online and discuss the following questions with your classmates

1) Do you think your lifestyle is energy efficient?
   e.g. Yes. I always use public transport, turn lights off when not in use, and always
      use my own bag.

2) Do you think people should cut down on the amount of
   meat they eat and perhaps eat more fish?
   e.g. I prefer meat than fish, but if it is more sustainable
      to eat fish. I think people should at least try to cut
      down on how much meat they eat.

4.1 Listen and fill in the blanks

Goal 12 Ensure sustainable consumption and production patterns

[as of 2019]

- At the moment the way we produce and (¹   ) plastic is not sustainable. In the past (²   ) years, our consumption and usage of plastic has (³   ) 20 times with (⁴   ) million tons of plastic being produced a year. That is a lot of plastic. What happens, however, when we (⁵   ) of this plastic? Where does it go? Plastic litter, such as single-use straws, plastic bags, bottles and food packaging, can (⁶   ) in our oceans. Around (⁷   ) billion pounds or just over 8 billion kilos of plastic is (⁸   ) to be in the sea. This has a profound effect on marine life. In March 2019, a washed-up dead whale was found in the Philippines with 40 kilos of plastic in its (⁹   ).

- Plastic is not biodegradable. This means that it is not able to decompose or be (¹⁰   ) down through bacteria or other (¹¹   ) organisms. Instead, once plastic is made and used, it is with us for generations. For example, the plastic bottles to be used (¹²   ) after you drink something, can take at least 450 years to (¹³   ). We can, of course, recycle plastic, but from the estimated 8.3 billion tons of plastic created in the last 70 years, only 9 % has been (¹⁴   ). Now, only a small amount of plastic is being recycled and most of it ends up in (¹⁵   ) and the ocean.

- One of the reasons why we have so much plastic pollution is because the plastic we create and (¹⁶   ) is used only once or for the short term. A lot of this plastic cannot be recycled. There is a need to (¹⁷   ) the production of this single-use disposable (¹⁸   ). Try to imagine how much of this single-use disposable plastic you use in a week, and you might be (¹⁹   ).

4.2 Questions for discussion

1) Make a list of all the disposable plastic items you use (for example, plastic bottles).
2) How can we protect marine life from pollution?
3) Do you recycle? How do you recycle in your local community?
4) Do you agree with a charge for plastic carrier bags?

5 | Reading | Doing more and better with less

5.1 What do we need to do for sustainable consumption and development?

As the economy has grown, our social progress has developed. This has led to environmental damage, <u>where</u> water, food and energy consumption can be affected. The things we rely on in our lives could be at risk because of these environmental changes.

In order to keep creating this economic growth along with sustainable development, we need to reduce our ecological footprint. This can be done by reducing our resource consumption and changing how we consume the resources we have.

Unfortunately, we are polluting our water faster than nature can purify or clean it in lakes and rivers. Moreover, nearly one third of food produced is wasted. Our overall

ECOLOGICAL FOOTPRINT

| Americans 9.5 | Canadians 7.8 | Australians 7.1 | Britons 5.3 | Japanese 4.9 | Germans 4.2 | Chinese 2.1 | Africans/Indians/others 1 |

energy consumption also needs to be reduced. This can lead to a reduction in CO_2 emissions. Sustainable consumption and production means 'doing more and better with less.' We are responsible to future generations to leave the planet safe. This is the reason <u>why</u> we need to reduce our resource consumption and waste.

What can we do to ensure sustainable consumption and production patterns? Reducing, reusing and recycling are probably things that we can do. This can be done by not wasting food, by reducing the use of plastic which is one of the main pollutants of our oceans, and by recycling and reusing what you used.

It is also important to beware what you buy. For example, we can reduce the amount of meat we eat. The demand for meat is increasing and global production of meat is set to double by 2050. This will have a huge impact on resources. Beef, for example, needs around 20 times more land to produce and emits 20 times more greenhouse gas emissions than plant proteins such as beans.

5.2 Discussion points

1) How can we reduce our ecological footprint?
2) Do you waste food? Do you have an eco-friendly lifestyle?
3) Do you use plastic bags at supermarkets or convenience stores?
4) Do you think you could give up eating beef?

Grammar point　relative adverbs（関係副詞）

下線部 where, when, why は関係副詞で、場所、時、理由などを表し、接続詞＋副詞の働きをします。たとえば when は時を示す語が先行詞になります。（➡文法マスター参照）

　　e.g. This is the time **when** we need to think about our environment.

6　Basic grammar exercises: relative adverbs

6.1　Choose the appropriate answer

1) We are living in a time (where / why / when) plastic causes problems.
2) We know the reasons (where / why / when) our oceans are polluted.
3) The ocean is a place (where / why / when) many kinds of marine life live.
4) Our food is produced in countries (where / why / when) people don't eat enough.

6.2　Read aloud the text and see how the relative adverb is used

Do you know any place where most of our plastic rubbish goes? I think the place where a lot of rubbish goes in is in landfills. There are many reasons why our oceans are polluted. Can you name three of them? I think the biggest reason why our oceans are polluted is because of the amount of plastic that is dumped into them.

6.3　Discussion: Do you use a lot of plastic in your daily life?

7　Reading graphs and charts

Check how relative adverbs are used and discuss E-waste in groups.

E-waste refers to various forms of electric and electronic equipment in your house, where you will not use them anymore. E-waste products have lost their utility value due to redundancy, replacement or breakage. Examples of E-waste includes refrigerators, washing machines, microwaves, televisions, radios, computers, and cell phones.

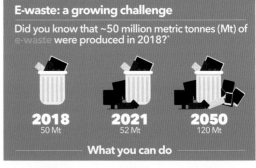

https://www.itu.int/en/sustainable-world/Pages/goal12.aspx

8 Research

Try to do some research and make a presentation using slides, a poster or a handout

Tips for doing your research

1) Define the term(s), such as responsible production and consumption
2) Identify the problems of responsible production and consumption that SDG 12 shows
3) Examine the realities around you with regards to SDG 12
4) Check the local or global efforts that aim to achieve SDG 12
5) Explain what you can do to achieve SDG 12
6) Refer to the local policies that aim to solve the problems of responsible production and consumption
7) Propose your own ideas or actions to solve these problems

Sample poster

How the ecological footprint works

Sustainable consumption and production / Doing more and better with less

The ecological footprint is the only metric that measures:
1. How much nature we have (the supply side)
2. How much nature we use (the demand side)

1. Biocapacity	**2. Natural resources**
cropland, grazing land, forest land, fishing grounds, and built-up land	plant-based food and products, livestock and fish products, timber and other forest products, and space for urban infrastructure

The Ecological Footprint
MEASURES
how fast we consume resources and generate waste

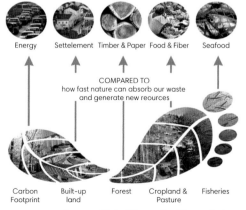

Energy   Settelement   Timber & Paper   Food & Fiber   Seafood

COMPARED TO
how fast nature can absorb our waste
and generate new reources

Carbon   Built-up   Forest   Cropland &   Fisheries
Footprint   land   Pasture

Source: Global Footprint Network, https://www.footprintnetwork.org

Unit 11 Climate Action

気候変動に具体的な対策を

Goal 13 Take urgent action to combat climate change and its impacts

1 Background (facts & figures)

Which facts and figures are you interested in?

- Carbon dioxide concentrations in the air are **146 %** of pre-industrial levels, and they are driving climate change.
- The global mean temperature in 2018 was **about one degree** above the pre-industrial baseline.

2 Topic-related vocabulary check

CD 2-10
↓ 033

2.1 Listen and fill in the blanks

words	meaning
sea level *n.*	the average (　　　　) of the sea [= 高さ]
drought *n.*	a long period of (　　　　) weather when there is not enough water for plants and animals to live [= 乾燥した]
extinction *n.*	a situation where an animal or a plant stops (　　　　) [= 存在する]
emit *v.*	to send out (　　　　), heat, light, sound, and so on into the air [= ガス]
greenhouse gas *n.*	a gas that stops (　　　　) from leaving the atmosphere and causes the greenhouse effect [= 熱]
trap *v.*	to (　　　　) something such as gas or water from getting away [= 妨げる]
melt *v.*	to become (　　　　) [= 液体]
flooding *n.*	a situation in which an area of land becomes covered with (　　　　) [= 水]
deplete *v.*	to (　　　　) the amount of something that is present or available [= 減らす]

2.2 Ask each other in pairs

> A: What does "emit" mean? Please explain it to me.
>
> B: "Emit" means to send out gas, heat and light, sound, and so on into the air.

3 Knowledge check (quiz)

3.1 Look up the answer online

1) Greenhouse gas concentrations in the air reached ___ percent of pre-industrial (1880–1900) levels in 2017.

   a) 35   b) 78   c) 146

2) Where did world leaders agree to a climate change deal in 2015?

   a) In Paris (Paris Agreement).

   b) In Kyoto (Kyoto Agreement).

   c) In New York (The Manhattan Agreement).

3) Sea levels have risen by about ___ cm since 1880 and are predicted to rise another 30 to 122 cm by 2100.

   a) 5   b) 13   c) 20

4) Which of these countries emits carbon dioxide most?

   a) The U.S.   b) China.   c) Russia.   d) Japan.

5) What is caused by the increase in atmospheric CO_2?

   a) Sea level rise.

   b) Heavy rain and drought.

   c) Temperature rise.

   d) Extinction of wildlife species.

   e) All of the above.

3.2 Do some research online and discuss the following questions with your classmates

1) Who should be in charge of looking after our planet earth?

   e.g. I think scientists, famous people or governments should be, but all of us live on this planet, so we should be all responsible for global warming and air pollution.

2) Do you think wasting less food is a way to reduce greenhouse gas emissions?

   e.g. Yes. I did research on food waste and global warming. I realize CO_2 is always emitted. I think we need to think more carefully about food waste.

4.1 Listen and fill in the blanks

Goal 13 Take urgent action to combat climate change and its impacts

- Climate change is the (^{1}) effects in global temperature. Although the Earth's climate has changed (^{2}) history, the Earth's average temperature has been (^{3}) rising since the mid-20th century compared to many other times. Greenhouse gases such as (^{4}) are thought to be the most significant (^{5}) of climate change.

- The greenhouse gases are (^{6}) in large part by human activities such as burning (^{7}). They trap solar (^{8}) and keep heat close to the Earth's (^{9}) rather than letting it escape into space. When the amount of greenhouse gases increases, they will trap extra heat and raise the Earth's temperature. That (^{10}) of heat is called the greenhouse effect.

- There are four major greenhouse gases. Carbon dioxide is the main greenhouse gas which comes from burning (^{11}), oil, gas and solid waste. Methane is released from a cow's burp, (^{12}) of organic waste in landfills, and natural gas. Nitrous oxide is released from bacteria in (^{13}). Modern agriculture and livestock, including (^{14}), manure, and burning of the agricultural residues, are the sources of nitrous oxide. Chlorofluorocarbon is one of the industrial gases used in a (^{15}) and an air-conditioner.

- Greenhouse effects could have huge impacts on us. Rising sea levels due to the (^{16}) of the ice sheets contributes to more (^{17}) storms and erosion. Warming ocean temperatures hurt most ocean dwellers and make frequent hurricanes. Heavy (^{18}) leads to flooding. Warming temperatures cause infectious diseases to spread to many areas of the world and also proliferate (^{19}) and diseases that affect many (^{20}).

4.2 Questions for discussion
1) What do you think about global warming? Are you worried about it?
2) Do you understand how the greenhouse effect occurs?
3) Are you contributing to greenhouse gases?
4) What do you know about the impact of the greenhouse effect?

5 Reading | Fossil fuel divestment

5.1 Do you know about fossil fuel divestment?

Divestment is the opposite of investment. It means to remove your money from stocks, bonds or funds. Fossil fuel divestment is a global movement. It asks institutions, universities, local authorities and pension funds to move their stocks, bonds or investment capitals out of fossil fuel related companies. It also asks them to re-invest their money in sustainable projects, climate action and non-fossil fuel related companies.

The fossil fuel companies play a huge role in CO_2 emissions causing global warming. Divesting from the fossil fuel companies, therefore, has serious implications and impact. Not only institutions but also individuals can take action in the world to ensure that their money should not be used to fund projects and industries for global warming. As of 2020, over 1,200 institutions and 58,000 individuals representing about 14 trillion dollars in assets worldwide divested from fossil fuel companies, according to 350.org (https://350.org).

You may feel that you have nothing to do with investment. However, part of your money at a bank might be used to invest in fossil fuel related companies. For that reason, there is the potential to be able to contribute to this movement on the individual level. For example, you can just withdraw your personal finances from fossil fuel-related institutions and reinvest them in local businesses, not-for-profit credit unions or clean energy future.

It is important to slow down global warming. Not using fossil fuels could be one of the greatest ideas to drastically transform business models of fossil fuel companies which exhaust limited fossil fuel reserves.

OVERVIEW

Totals

$6.09 Trillion

Approx. Value of Institutions Divesting

How is this number calculated?

852

Institutions Divesting

58,000+

Individuals divesting about $5.2 Billion

What kinds of Institutions are divesting?

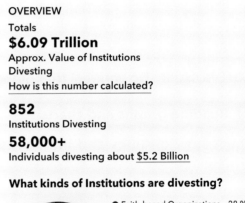

● Faith-based Organizations	28 %
● Philanthropic Foundation	19 %
● Government	17 %
◐ Educational Institution	16 %
◔ NGO	5 %
◌ For Profit Corporation	3 %
● Healthcare Institution	1 %
● Cultural Institution	0 %
● Other	0 %

https://effectiveassets.com/fossil-fuel-divestment/

5.2 Discussion points

1) What is divestment?
2) Why is divestment important?
3) How many people and how much money were divested from fossil fuels in 2020?
4) How can divestment help reduce global warming?

Grammar point　gerunds and infinitives（動名詞・不定詞）

文中の下線部 diverting, not using は動名詞で、動詞に -ing をつけることで、また、to remove, to slow など
の to 不定詞も同様に名詞の働きをします。（➡文法マスター参照）

　e.g. **Understanding** the impacts of global warming is important.

6　Basic grammar exercises: gerunds and infinitives

6.1　Choose the appropriate answer

1) Energy companies ended up (wasting / to waste) $2.2 trillion in fossil fuel investments.
2) The Paris Agreement aims (to achieve / achieving) net zero emissions by 2100.
3) Many countries promised (to deploy / deploying) more clean energy.

6.2　Read aloud the text and see how gerunds and infinitives are used

Recently I often feel that global warming is occurring around me because of the heavy rain, storms and forest fires happening all around the world. Stopping global warming for the next generation is something we need to do. I think there are many things we can do now. For example, we can stop wasting food; we can avoid using cars, and use public transportation. We can also use renewable energy and invest our money in clean energy companies.

6.3　Discussion: Do you feel that global warming is happening around you?

7　Reading graphs and charts

Check how gerunds and infinitives are used and discuss CO_2 emission in groups

The graph shows the increasing CO_2 emissions by countries from 1970 to 2018. It seems difficult to decrease CO_2 emissions because they have grown steadily since 2000. China's CO_2 emissions in particular increased in 2016. This was mainly due to consuming a lot of oil and gas.

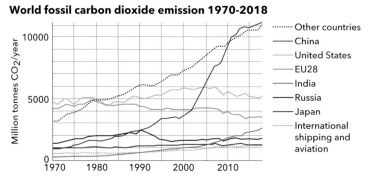

World fossil carbon dioxide emission 1970-2018

https://upload.wikimedia.org/wikipedia/commons/1/15/World_fossil_carbon_dioxide_emissions_six_top_countries_and_confederations.png

8　Research

Try to do some research and make a presentation using slides, a poster or a handout

Tips for doing your research

1) Define the term(s), such as climate change, greenhouse gases, and divestment
2) Identify the problems of global warming that SDG 13 shows
3) Examine the realities around you with regards to SDG 13
4) Check the local or global efforts that are being done to achieve SDG 13
5) Explain what you can do to achieve SDG 13
6) Refer to the local government policies that aim to to solve the problems of global warming
7) Propose your own ideas or actions to solve these problems

Sample

GLOBAL WARMING is happening

Sanshu Taro
CLIL University

1

Bush fires in Australia

2

Sea level is rising

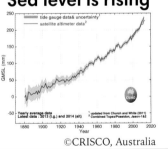

©CRISCO, Australia

3

What can we do to stop global warming?

4

- Voice your concerns
- Use renewable energy
- Think and buy energy-efficient appliances
- Reduce water waste
- Think about food loss
- Unplug devices
- Take public transportation

5

References

- https://climate.nasa.gov/vital-signs/sea-level/

- https://www.nrdc.org/stories/how-you-can-stop-global-warming

6

Unit 12 Life below Water / Life on Land

海の豊かさを守ろう・陸の豊かさも守ろう

Goal 14 Conserve and sustainably use the oceans, seas and marine resources for sustainable development

Goal 15 Protect, restore and promote sustainable use of terrestrial ecosystems, sustainably manage forests, combat desertification, and halt and reverse land degradation and halt biodiversity loss

1 Background (facts & figures)

Which facts and figures are you interested in?

- **One third of the world's marine fish stocks** are overfished today.

- Every year, **13 million hectares of forests** are being lost which is equivalent to **36 football fields per minute**.

2 Topic-related vocabulary check

CD 2-13
↓ 036

2.1 Listen and fill in the blanks

words	meaning
resource *n.*	something that exists in (　　　　　　) and can be used by people [＝自然]
habitat *n.*	the natural (　　　　　　) that an animal or plant usually lives in [＝環境]
ecosystem *n.*	all the living things that live in a particular area together with the (　　　　　) relationship [＝複雑な]
biodiversity *n.*	a wide (　　　　　) of plant and animal species that exist in a particular region and make a balanced environment [＝多様性]
livelihood *n.*	the (　　　　　) you earn the money you need to pay for food, a place to live, and clothing [＝方法]
degradation *n.*	the process of something being damaged or made (　　　　　) [＝より悪くする]

2.2 Ask each other in pairs

A: What does "degradation" mean? Please explain it to me.

B: "Degradation" means the process of something being damaged or made worse.

3.1 Look up the answer online

1) How many people depend on forests for their livelihood?
   a) Around 2.6 billion people do.
   b) Around 1.6 billion people do.
   c) Around 70 million people do.

2) What percentage of world oceans are heavily affected by human activities?
   a) More than 60 %.
   b) As much as 40 %.
   c) Only 20 %.

3) Do oceans absorb carbon dioxide produced by humans?
   a) Yes, they do. Oceans absorb about 30 % of carbon dioxide, buffering the impacts of global warming.
   b) No, they don't. Instead, forests absorb about 40 % of carbon dioxide created by humans.

4) We lost 15.8 million hectares of tropical rainforest in 2017. How many football fields of trees were lost every minute a year?
   a) Four football fields.
   b) Fourteen football fields.
   c) Forty football fields.

3.2 Do some research online and discuss the following questions with your classmates

1) Why do you think trees are important? Give as many reasons as you can.
   e.g. Trees clean the air we breathe and provide habitat to over 80 % of the world's terrestrial biodiversity.

2) Do you know what causes ocean pollution?
   e.g. Yes. I found out that billions of tons of trash enter the ocean.

4.1 Listen and fill in the blanks

CD 2-14
↓ 037

Goal 14 Conserve and sustainably use the oceans, seas and marine resources for sustainable development

- Oceans cover more than 70 percent of the (^{1}) of the Earth, and contain 97 percent of the planet's water. Oceans (^{2}) about (^{3}) of the oxygen we breathe, (^{4}) the global ecosystem by absorbing (^{5}) from the atmosphere, and (^{6}) about 30 percent of the carbon dioxide produced by humans.

- Oceans are (^{7}) for human well-being and social and economic development worldwide. Over 3 billion people depend on marine and (^{8}) resources for their livelihood. The market value of marine and coastal resources and industries is (^{9}) at 3 trillion dollars per year or about 5 percent of global GDP.

CD 2-15
↓ 038

Goal 15 Protect, restore and promote sustainable use of terrestrial ecosystems, sustainably manage forests, combat desertification, and halt and reverse land degradation and halt biodiversity loss

- Forests cover 30 percent of the surface of the Earth, and mountains (^{10}) 60 to 80 percent of the world's (^{11}). Every year, we lose 13 million hectares of (^{12}) that are home to more than (^{13}) percent of all terrestrial (^{14}) and provide livelihood to around 1.6 billion people.

- 2.6 billion people depend directly on (^{15}) for a living, but 52 percent of the land used for agriculture is (^{16}) or severely affected by soil (^{17}). Globally, 74 percent of the poor are directly affected by land degradation. An estimated 20 percent of the Earth's land area was degraded between 2000 and 2015.

4.2 Questions for discussion

1) Which SDG are you interested in, life below water or life on land?
2) Why are oceans and seas important to us?
3) Do you know what animals or what species of fish are endangered?
4) What can you do to conserve the oceans and manage forests?

5.1 Have you ever seen the blue MSC ecolabel?

©MSC

Oceans play an important role in providing nutritious food and good livelihoods. Around the world, more than a billion people rely on fish for their main source of protein. Around 1 in 10 people depend on fishing for their livelihood, and seafood is the most traded food in the world. Despite this importance, the world's marine and coastal resources are threatened by overfishing, pollution and habitat degradation.

Today, more than 30 percent of global fish stocks are overfished. Overfishing not only reduces food production and biodiversity, but it also impairs the functioning of ecosystems. Illegal, unreported and unregulated fishing makes matters worse. The way that seafood gets from the ocean to your plate is not so simple that you might eat illegal fish without realizing it. How do we know which seafood products are safer and more sustainable than other foods?

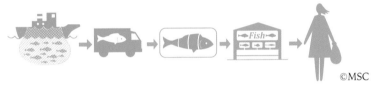
©MSC

The Marine Stewardship Council (MSC) sets a standard for sustainable fishing. This standard is used to check that 1) the fish stock is at healthy level, 2) impact of fishing on marine life and habitats is minimized, and 3) the effective management system exists and the fisheries comply with it. Once all these checks are satisfied, the fishery is certified. Any company which wants to sell certified products with MSC's little blue label needs a chain of custody certification for seafood traceability. It also makes sure that the MSC certified seafood is not mixed with non-certified seafood. By choosing seafood products with the blue MSC ecolabel, you can directly support fishing communities that take care of our oceans. Today, you can see the blue MSC ecolabel on fish sandwiches and rice balls. We have to think a lot more about fisheries than we have done before.

写真提供：日本マクドナルド

5.2 Discussion points

1) How many people eat fish in the world?
2) What does the blue MSC ecolabel mean?
3) Do you know where your seafood comes from?
4) What do you think about the ecolabeling system?

Grammar point comparatives（比較）

文中の下線部 more than, the most traded food, safer and more sustainable than などは、比較の表現です。
状態、様態、程度を表す形容詞、副詞に用いられます。（➡ 文法マスター参照）
> e.g. Rice is **as healthy as** bread.
>   Overfishing means fishing **harder than** needed.

6 Basic grammar exercises: comparatives

6.1 Choose the appropriate answer

1) Biodiversity is declining (as fast as / faster than / fastest) before.
2) The Amazon forest regrows much (as slow as / slower than / slowest) thought.
3) You drank (as much water as / water than / the most water) I did.
4) We should remove (as much plastic / more plastic than / the most plastic) as possible.

6.2 Read aloud the text and see how comparatives are used

To protect wildlife in the ocean and on land, you should use more renewable and recycled materials. Besides, you should eliminate more waste and make your lifestyle more affordable and sustainable. If you do this, you might be considered a good environmental citizen. I hope lots of people will do as much as they can.

6.3 Discussion: What are the causes of environmental change?

7 Reading graphs and charts

Check how comparatives are used and discuss the change in groups

Fish can spoil more quickly than many other foods these days. The global increase in food fish consumption was higher than population growth. Fish consumption per person grew from 9 kg in 1961 to 20.2 kg in 2015.

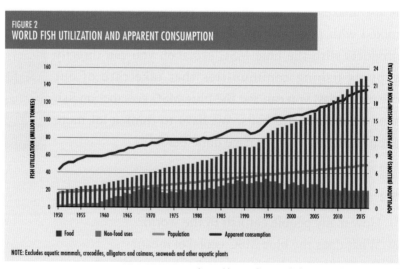

FIGURE 2
WORLD FISH UTILIZATION AND APPARENT CONSUMPTION

NOTE: Excludes aquatic mammals, crocodiles, alligators and caimans, seaweeds and other aquatic plants

■ Food   ■ Non-food uses   — Population   — Apparent consumption

http://www.fao.org/3/i9540en/I9540EN.pdf

8 | Research

Try to do some research and make a presentation using slides, a poster or a handout

Tips for doing your research

1) Define the term(s), such as ecolabel and biodiversity
2) Identify the problems of life below water and life on land that SDG 14 and SDG 15 show
3) Examine the realities around you with regards to SDG 14 and SDG 15
4) Check the local or global efforts that are being done to achieve SDG 14 and SDG 15
5) Explain what you can do to achieve SDG 14 and SDG 15
6) Refer to the local policies that aim to solve the problems of life below water and life on land
7) Propose your own ideas or actions to solve these problems

Sample

Rainforest Alliance Certification

CLIL University
Sanshu Hana

1

Deforestation

- Nearly half of the world's forests have been lost.
- Each year additional 32 million acres are destroyed.
- Many of Earth's plants and animals will be endangered.

2

Forests are important

- Source of air, water and food
- Shelter
- Livelihoods for 1.6 billion people
- 80 percent of the world's terrestrial biodiversity

3

Rainforest Alliance Certification

- increase productivity
- improve farmer incomes

Profit

People
- promote rights of rural people
- provide a decent life for all

Planet
- use land and water carefully
- protect natural resources

Source: Rainforest Alliance   4

Certified Products

The little green frog symbol can be found on farm and forest products around the world.

- Banana
- Cocoa
- Coffee
- Tea etc.

Source: Rainforest Alliance   5

References and Websites

Rainforest Alliance
https://www.rainforest-alliance.org/

Food and Agriculture Organization of the United Nations
http://www.fao.org/home/en/

WWF
https://wwf.panda.org/

6

Unit 13 Peace, Justice and Strong Institutions

平和と公正をすべての人に

Goal 16 Promote peaceful and inclusive societies for sustainable development, provide access to justice for all and build effective, accountable and inclusive institutions at all levels

1 Background (facts & figures)

Which facts and figures are you interested in?

- **70 % of detected victims** of human trafficking are women and girls.
- From January to October 2018, the UN recorded and verified **397 killings** of human rights defenders, journalists, and trade unionists across **41 countries**.

2 Topic-related vocabulary check

CD 2-17
↓ 040

2.1 Listen and fill in the blanks

words	meaning
human trafficking *n.*	taking people to another country and forcing them to (　　　　　) [= 働く]
human rights *n.*	the basic rights every person should have to be treated in a (　　　　　) equal way [= 公正な]
persecution *n.*	cruel or (　　　　　) treatment of people, especially because of their religious or political beliefs [= 不公平な]
conflict *n.*	a state of disagreement, argument, (　　　　　) or war between people, groups, countries, etc. [= 争い]
homicide *n.*	the crime of (　　　　　) [= 殺人]
refugee *n.*	someone who has been forced to leave the country, especially during a (　　　　) [= 戦争]
sexual exploitation *n.*	a situation in which someone is forced to have sexual (　　　　　) with someone else [= 関係]
abduct *v.*	to take someone (　　　　　) by force [= 離れて]
victim *n.*	someone who (　　　　　) because of something bad that happens [= 苦しむ]

2.2 Ask each other in pairs

A : What does "human trafficking" mean? Please explain it to me.

B : "Human trafficking" means taking people to another country and forcing them to work.

3 Knowledge check (quiz)

3.1 Look up the answer online

1) What is the number of people fleeing war, persecution and conflict in 2018?
   a) Over 7 million people.
   b) Over 70 million people.
   c) Over 700 million people.

2) Which of the following areas had the highest homicide rate between 2007 and 2017?
   a) Sub-Saharan Africa.
   b) North America.
   c) Latin America and the Caribbean.

3) How did the number of trafficking victims per country change between 2010 and 2016?
   a) It increased by more than 100.
   b) It decreased by more than 100.
   c) It stayed almost the same.

4) What is the percentage of children under 5 who have registered their births in sub-Saharan Africa?
   a) About 45 %.
   b) About 60 %.
   c) About 75 %.

5) How many female human rights defenders, journalists and trade unionists were killed worldwide in 2018?
   a) 9.   b) 22.   c) 39.

3.2 Do some research online and discuss the following questions with your classmates

1) What are the causes of wars?
   e.g. Some wars are caused for territorial or economic gains.

2) What is the purpose of human trafficking?
   e.g. Some children may be trafficked and forced to work with a very low wage.

4.1 Listen and fill in the blanks

Goal 16 Promote peaceful and inclusive societies for sustainable development, provide access to justice for all and build effective, accountable and inclusive institutions at all levels

- Refugees are people who have (^{1}) from their own country for several reasons. Reasons include wars, civil wars, and political or religious (^{2}). According to UNHCR, at the end of 2018, 6.7 million refugees were from Syria, where the civil war between the (^{3}) forces and anti-government groups has (^{4}) since 2011. Other countries with a large number of (^{5}) are Afghanistan (2.7 million), South Sudan (2.3 million), Myanmar (1.1 million), and Somalia (0.9 million).

- The number of human trafficking (^{6}) detected in 2016 was (^{7}). About 70 % of them were women and girls, most of whom were trafficked for sexual (^{8}). In addition, many children were trafficked for forced (^{9}). In both cases, the victims were usually forced to live and work under very bad (^{10}) in terms of food, shelter, and (^{11}).

- In order for people to live in (^{12}), it is very important for every country to establish national human rights institution(s) (NHRIs). Based on the so-called Paris (^{13}) resolved at the United Nations (^{14}) in 1993, each UN member state is required to establish an NHRI independent of its government, and more than 100 NHRIs have been (^{15}) in the world so far. (^{16}), however, is one of the few countries that has not yet established an NHRI, and the Japan Federation of Bar Associations and other groups, as (^{17}) as the United Nations Human Rights Committee, have been (^{18}) the Japanese government to establish an independent NHRI as soon as possible.

©UNCHR

4.2 Questions for discussion

1) What are the major causes of the refugee problem?
2) What are the serious problems refugees have? What kind of assistance do they need?
3) What do you think about the fact that the major reason for trafficking is sexual exploitation?
4) What can you do to eradicate sexual exploitation?

5 Reading | Child soldiers

5.1 Do you know there are many child soldiers around the world?

It is said that many children are recruited and used as child soldiers in armed conflicts around the world. Armed groups recruit boys and girls as young soldiers or servants, often in very violent ways.

Onimaru and Ogawa (2005) tells the story of a boy named Charles, who became a young soldier of an anti-government group called Lord's Resistance Army (LRA) in Uganda. He was once abducted by some members of LRA, then taken back to his house, told to cut off his mother's arm, and taken again to their base. Forced to fight against the government forces for three years, Charles was able to come back to his home village.

According to Onimaru and Ogawa, such armed groups practice some ways to make it very difficult for boys and girls to escape, such as threating, the use of alcohol and drugs, and brainwashing. Girls may be forced to get married to member soldiers and give birth to babies, who in turn may be raised as members of the group. In addition, poverty may force them to stay in the groups so that they can at least get enough food to live. A lack of people's understanding and acceptance may also have negative effects on the child soldiers' returning to their home community.

Some NGOs are working hard to get former child soldiers back to their community and encourage them to live peaceful lives. The NGOs also provide them with basic education so that they can work and earn money to live, and they give psychotherapy, because they have suffered serious trauma caused by horrible experiences. The fundamental solution is, however, to stop war and conflict around the world. As global citizens, we all must think about how we can realize a peaceful world.

* 鬼丸昌也・小川真吾 （2005）「ぼくは 13 歳 職業、兵士。——あなたが戦争のある村で生まれたら」合同出版

©AFP ＝時事

5.2 Discussion points

1) Where are wars and conflicts happening in the world now?

2) Why do armed groups recruit child soldiers? What are the advantages of recruiting children, compared to recruiting adults?

3) What kind of help do former child soldiers need?

Grammar point　articles（冠詞）

文中の下線部 **a, an, the** は冠詞です。初めて話題に上る単数形の名詞には不定冠詞 **a/an**（特定できない中の一つ）、すでに話し手・聞き手双方に認識されているものを示す名詞には定冠詞 **the** が使われます。（➡文法マスター参照）

e.g. I visited **a** small village four years ago. I saw **a** lot of broken houses and buildings in **the** village.

6　Basic grammar exercises: articles

6.1　Choose the appropriate answer

1) There is (an / the) armed group called LRA. (A / The) boy named Charles was abducted by (a / the) group ten years ago.

2) Lucy was 13 years old when she was kidnaped by a violent extremist group. Right after she was kidnaped, she was forced to get married to (a / the) soldier in (a / the) same group.

3) (A / The) government of Japan has not yet established (a / the) national human rights institute (NHRI) independent of the government.

6.2　Read aloud the text and see how articles are used

The Rohingya are a Muslim ethnic group in Western Myanmar, and they have been suffering from persecution and discrimination by the local people and troops. A severe armed conflict occurred in 2017, and the conflict forced more than 900,000 Rohingya people to flee from the area they lived in. Most of them are now living at refugee camps in Bangladesh, but the living conditions are awful.

6.3　Discussion: What do you think you can do for Rohingya people?

7　Reading graphs and charts

Check how articles are used and discuss refugee problems in groups

The number of people who escaped war, persecution and conflict exceeded 70 million in 2018. It is the highest level that the organization has seen in its almost 70 year history. The number of people who have been forcibly displaced is twice the level of 20 years ago. In 2018, 57 percent of all refugees came from three countries - Syria, Afghanistan and South Sudan.

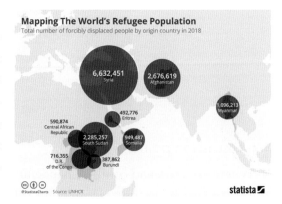

https://www.statista.com/chart/18436/total-number-of-refugees-by-origin-country/

8 Research

Try to do some research and make a presentation using slides, a poster or a handout

𝕋𝕚𝕡𝕤 for doing your research

1) Define the term(s), such as refugees, human trafficking, and birth registration
2) Identify the problems of peace, justice, and strong institutions that SDG 16 shows
3) Examine the realities around you with regards to SDG 16
4) Check the local or global efforts that are being done to achieve SDG 16
5) Explain what you can do to achieve SDG 16
6) Refer to the local policies that aim to solve the problems of peace, justice, and strong institutions
7) Propose your own ideas or actions to solve these problems

Sample

Accepting more refugees in Japan

Sanshu Taro
CLIL University

1

Refugees around the world

Mapping The World's Refugee Population
Total number of forcibly displaced people by origin country in 2018

6,632,451 Syria
2,676,619 Afghanistan

Over 70 million people are fleeing from war, persecution and conflict

statista

2

Acceptance of refugees in Japan

Year	Applicants	Admitted as refugees
2013	3260	6
2014	5000	11
2015	7586	27
2016	10901	28
2017	19629	20
2018	10493	42
2019	10375	44

Source: 外務省 3

Accepting refugees in other countries

Country	Refugees accepted
Turkey	3,700,000
Pakistan	1,400,000
Uganda	1,200,000
Sudan	1,100,000
Germany	1,100,000
Japan	44

Source: UNHCR 4

Problems in accepting refugees in Japan

- Geographical distance
- Overly strict examination
- Assistance for refugees
  - Social services
  - Education
  - Job opportunities
  - Mutual understanding in the community

5

What we can do

- Get to know more about refugees
  - Study / Research
  - Read books about refugees
  - Watch movies
  - Talk directly with refuges
- Language assistance
- Education assistance

6

---

http://www.moj.go.jp/content/001317678.pdf   https://www.unhcr.org/figures-at-a-glance.html

Unit 14 — Partnerships for the Goals

パートナーシップで目標を達成しよう

Goal 17 Strengthen the means of implementation and revitalize the global partnership for sustainable development

1 Background (facts & figures)

Which facts and figures are you interested in?

• At the end of 2018, **more than half the world's population** had access to the Internet. **Over 86 %** in developed countries were online, compared with **47 %** in developing countries.

• Net ODA flows **totaled $149 billion** in 2018, **down 2.7 %** from 2017. It was largely due to a reduction in donor country aid for hosting refugees.

2 Topic-related vocabulary check

CD 2-20
↓ 043

2.1 Listen and fill in the blanks

words	meaning
digital divide *n.*	the gap that exists between ( ) who can use the ICT and those who can't [= 人々]
remittance *n.*	money that is ( ) by foreign workers back to family or others in their own country [= 送る]
income *n.*	money that you ( ) from your work or receive from investments [= 稼ぐ]
private sector *n.*	the part of the economy that is ( ) and run by a private company [= 所有する]
ODA *n.*	official development assistance to promote the ( ) development and welfare of developing countries [= 経済的な]
net ODA *n.*	grants or loans to ( ) countries [= 開発途上の]
public-private partnership (PPP) *n.*	a ( ) project between two or more public and private sectors [= 共同の]

2.2 Ask each other in pairs

A: What does "remittance" mean? Please explain it to me.

B: "Remittance" means money that is sent by foreign workers back to family or others in their own country.

3 Knowledge check (quiz)

3.1 Look up the answer online

1) What does "multilateral aid" refer to?
   a) Assistance through international organizations.
   b) Assistance through NGOs.
   c) Assistance through individuals.

©Yukiko Abe

2) What does "a private sector or company" refer to?
   a) The Japanese government.
   b) The World Bank.
   c) Panasonic Corporation.

3) Remittances will be the _____ source of external financing in low-and middle-income countries in 2019.
   a) largest   b) lowest   c) highest

4) In 2019, annual remittance flows to low- and middle-income countries are projected to reach _____ dollars.
   a) 550 billion   b) 50 billion   c) 5 billion

5) What is "South-South cooperation (SSC)"?
   a) The technical cooperation among developing countries.
   b) The technical cooperation between developing countries and developed countries.
   c) The technical cooperation among countries in the Southern Hemisphere.

3.2 Do some research online and discuss the following questions with your classmates

1) Why do private sectors or companies actively commit to global issues and SDGs?
   e.g. They have knowledge, products and human resources. They can contribute to addressing global issues and do business in the world.

2) Why are remittances needed especially in low income countries?
   e.g. In low income countries, unemployment rates are higher, so people want to move to other countries to earn money.

4.1 Listen and fill in the blanks

Goal 17 Strengthen the means of implementation and revitalize the global partnership for sustainable development

- We need to have a (^{1}) commitment to partnership and cooperation to achieve this goal. We will need (^{2}) policies, first. Then we will make a good environment for sustainable development at all (^{3}) and by all actors. In addition, we need to have a global partnership. Towards this end, we have identified some areas as critical, such as technology, trade, (^{4}), monitoring, and accountability.

- Project Everyone was devised by Richard Curtis, a (^{5}) and founder of Comic Relief. He has been working closely with the United Nations to (^{6}) the SDGs. The initiative contributed to the design of the (^{7}), graphics and the short names for each goal in order to make them as clear and useful for (^{8}) as possible. Each logo has a (^{9}) and message.

- The #HelloGlobalGoals collaboration with Sanrio Co., Ltd. aims to raise (^{10}) of the SDGs among Hello Kitty's fans worldwide through a monthly series of YouTube videos. Launched in (^{11}) 2019, during the High-Level Debate of the General Assembly, the SDG-themed videos continue to be (^{12}) on Hello Kitty's global channel. They show Kitty (^{13}) about the SDGs from UN (^{14}) and traveling to different parts of the world to see actual UN projects.

- Many (^{15}) contribute to the SDGs. Piko Taro, an entertainer (^{16}) for his viral music video "Pen-Pineapple-Apple-Pen" (PPAP), has joined the ranks of celebrities who (^{17}) the SDGs. In 2017, when Piko Taro visited the United Nations, he presented both his PPAP (^{18}) song and the rearranged version titled "Public-(^{19}) Action for Partnership (PPAP)".

4.2 Questions for discussion

1) What is the advantage of having a partnership for achieving this SDG?
2) How do Hello Kitty and Piko Taro contribute to and promote the SDGs?
3) Do you have any ideas to motivate people to think about the earth, environment, vulnerable people and countries?
4) What can you do to achieve this SDG by 2030?

5 Reading | Public-private-partnerships (PPPs)

5.1 PPPs can provide public services and improve efficiency and service

Public Private Partnerships (PPPs) are long-term contracts between public sectors and private companies in the hope that private companies will finance public sectors which have been hit by the financial crisis. They aim to provide public services, like education and transportation, and improve efficiency and service qualitatively and quantitatively. PPPs don't intend to change the private business into a government-operated service.

The model of PPPs is very flexible and visible in a variety of forms. For instance, some PPPs have been concerned with the delivery service for the public sector by a private sector under a long-term agreement. Agreements for many Private Finance Initiative (PFI) projects have now been signed in numerous sectors, including health, education, transport, information and communication technology (ICT), environment, and accommodation. In March 2016, there were 527 PFI/PPP projects in Japan. This is double the number of projects compared to 10 years ago. These projects are currently involved in a number of primary operations and management of public services, such as medical facilities, cultural centers, and waste treatment plants. PFI/PPP projects awarded in concession are still in the minority, with only 13 being awarded or imminent.

The GHIT (Global Health Innovative Technology) fund is a Japanese-led initiative aiming to discover and advance the development of new health technologies. In 2016, the GHIT fund announced that it was investing in a vaccine that could block the transmission of two species of malaria. Its main role is to invest in the development of products for infectious diseases prevalent in developing countries. In 2017, Dr. Naoko Yamamoto, Senior Assistant Minister for Global Health, Ministry of Health, Labour and Welfare, said, "I highly value the steady progress of GHIT so far. I also feel that we have fostered a trust between the public and private sectors in the process."

5.2 Discussion points

1) What are PPPs?
2) What is the model of PPPs?
3) What kind of PFI/PPP projects are there in Japan? What projects are you interested in?
4) What do you think about the private sectors' contribution to SDGs?

Grammar point　direct and reported speech（直接話法・間接話法）

文中の下線部 GHIT Found announced, Dr. Naoko Yamato said は、間接話法 (reported speech)、直接話法（direct speech）を導いています。直接話法は発話をそのまま伝え、間接話法は内容を伝えます。（➡文法マスター参照）

e.g. She said to us, "I will contribute to SDGs proactively."

She told us **that** she would contribute to SDGs proactively.

6　Basic grammar exercises: direct and reported speech

6.1　Choose the appropriate answer

1) She said, "I will work for the UN."

= She said that (I / she) would work for the UN.

2) She said to me, "Where do you live?"

= She asked me (where I lived / where he lived).

3) He said to us, "Do you agree with SDG 17?"

= He asked us (that we / if we) agreed with SDG 17.

4) They shouted to her, "Don't come!" = They shouted to her (not to / don't) come.

6.2　Read aloud the text and see how direct and reported speech is used

Dr. Tetsu Nakamura, a Japanese physician and humanitarian, explained of his belief, "we do not necessarily have a firm philosophy about what an aid organization should do." "What is very clear to me, however," he added, "is that we must view things from the local people's perspective and respect their culture and values." He believed that helping the people in this way would truly benefit them.

6.3　Discussion: What do you think about Dr. Tetsu Nakamura?

7　Reading graphs and charts

Check how direct and reported speech is used and discuss the Internet in groups

In developed countries, most people are online. 86.6 % of individuals use the Internet. They say, "You cannot work without the Internet." However, in the least developed countries (LDCs), only 19.1 % of individuals are online in 2019. Africa is the region with the lowest Internet users. Research suggests that Internet uses are growing across sub-Saharan Africa but most are still offline.

Most of the offline population lives in least developed countries

Percentage of individuals using the Internet, by region and development status, 2019*

Region	%
Europe	82.5
The Americas	77.2
CIS	72.2
Asia & Pacific	48.4
Arab States	51.6
Africa	28.2
World	53.6
Developed	86.6
Developing	47.0
LDCs	19.1

Developed Countries 86.6%

LDCs 19.1%

Note: * ITU estimate. Source: ITU

https://www.itu.int/en/ITU-D/Statistics/Documents/facts/FactsFigures2019.pdf

90

8 Research

Try to do some research and make a presentation using slides, a poster or a handout

🆃🅸🅿🆂 for doing your research

1) Define the terms, such as partnership and PPPs
2) Identify the problems of partnership, capacity-development and technology transfer that SDG 17 shows
3) Examine the realities around you with regards to SDG 17
4) Check your local or global efforts to achieve SDG 17
5) Explain what you can do to achieve SDG 17
6) Refer to the local policies that aim to solve the problems of partnership
7) Propose your own ideas or actions to solve these problems

Sample

Partnership for the SDGs

©UN Photo / Cia Pak   1

Who are the actors for the SDGs?

- Public Sectors
- Private Sectors
- Academia
- NGOs and NPOs
- Others

2

Why do we need partnership to achieve the SDGs?

- Share knowledge and skills
- Enhance capacities
- Strengthen resources, organization and systems
- Create innovation
- Create new synergy effect
- Crete momentum toward "social good" etc.

3

To understand partnership, let's check the following words

- CSR ： Corporate Social Responsibility
- PRI: Principle for Responsible Investment
- ESG: Environment, Social and Governance
- CSV: Creating Shared Value
- PPP: Public Private Partnership
- SSC: South–South cooperation

4

Transformation of Business

Core business for SDGs

2011 CSV

2006 CSR PRI and ESG Investment

5

Let's find an example of partnership from the SDGs online platform

6

スライド・ポスター作成方法
How to make slides and a poster

スライドを使いプレゼンテーションをする際の基本手順と効果的なスライドの作成方法に従い、スライドを作成してみよう。

1 **プレゼンテーション・スライド作成の基本的手順と例**

① **最初のスライド**：プレゼンテーションのタイトル、自分の所属と名前、メールアドレス、プレゼンテーションの日付、授業科目名等を入れる。

② **2枚目のスライド**：outline として、プレゼンテーションの流れ、または目次を入れる。

③ **3枚目のスライド**：introduction（導入）を入れ、問題提起や聞き手に質問などを投げかけることにより、聞き手を引き付ける。

④ **4枚目のスライドから**：outline に沿って、プレゼンテーションを進める。

⑤ **プレゼンテーションの最後**：必ず conclusion（結論）を入れ、プレゼンテーションで言いたかったことを簡潔にまとめる。

⑥ **最後に**：引用した書籍やウェブサイトなどあれば、References（参考文献）として入れる。

（例）

**DO YOU KNOW
FOOD BANK?**

CLIL University
Sanshu Hana

1

Outline

1. Introduction
2. Food Bank
3. Advantages and Disadvantages
4. Conclusion
5. References

2

Introduction

Have you heard about food loss?

3

Conclusion

- The food bank may solve the problems of hunger in the world.

- Let's think about what we can do every day for achieving SDGs!

4

2 | スライド作成のポイント

① 伝えたいメッセージを短く一言に

スライドは、「読ませるもの」ではなく、「見せる」ものであるため、一つのスライドには、伝えたいメッセージを短く一言にまとめる。プレゼンテーション資料と同じ内容の長い文で構成されたスライドでは、聞き手は、読むことに集中してしまうため、プレゼンテーションを聞き逃してしまう。

② 一つのスライドに、一つのメッセージ

複数のメッセージを一つのスライドに入れると、内容が複雑になり、プレゼンターが、何を本当に言いたいことなのか、聞き手が混乱してしまい、わからなくなる。原則として、一つのスライドには、一つのメッセージを入れる。スライドが複数になっても構わない。

③ スライドの流れを論理的に

スライドを作成後、話の流れが論理的かどうか、聞き手にわかりやすいかどうかを何度も確認する。また、結論との整合性も確認する。後で、資料だけを見ても、内容や結論が正しく伝わるように簡潔に作成する。

④ レイアウトを工夫

スライドのタイトルやメッセージの位置、サイズを統一し、同じグループの情報は近くにまとめて配列する。

⑤ テキスト

文字の大きさ、書体（フォント）、書式、色を統一させる。色数はできるだけ少なくし、文字の装飾機能は、限定的にする。黄色など、見えにくい色は使用しないようにする。

⑥ 図やグラフ

文字や数字だけでなく、図、グラフ、表、イラストや写真を活用することにより、聞き手によりイメージを伝えやすくなる。しかし、一枚にたくさんの写真やイラストを使うと見えづらくなるため、余白を生かす程度に控えめに使う。また、背景に画像やイラストをなるべく入れないようにする。

⑦ 画面切り替えとアニメーション

原則として、画面の切り替えとアニメーションは必要ないが、聞き手の興味や注意をひくためやアクセントをつけるために効果的な場合もある。しかし、頻繁に使いすぎないほうがよい。

⑧ スライド番号とスライド合計

スライドに、スライド番号とスライドの合計を入れる。スライド番号は質疑応答の際やプレゼンテーションの時間の目安を知るのに効果的である。

ポスター発表とは、大判のポスターの前で行うプレゼンテーションの一形式である。基本的には、スライドを使ったプレゼンテーションと似ているが、同時に発表を行う点や発表者と聞き手が対話を行えるなど異なる点もある。次のポスターの作成のポイントを踏まえ、ポスター発表をしてみよう。

① **タイトルが大事**

見る人を引き付けるような短く、簡潔な新聞の見出しのようなタイトルをつける。

② **タイトルや見出しの文字は大きくする**

文字ポイント数の目安：A0 サイズ（118.9 × 84.1cm）の場合

タイトル 100 ／発表者名 55 ／見出し 60

③ **ポスターと論文 (レポート) は似ている**

レポートや論文のように、概要、序論、疑問、目的 (仮説)、結果、考察、結論、参考文献をはっきりと書くこと。序論と結論を対応させる。

④ **ポスターはレポートとは似ていない点もある**

論文やレポートと異なり、ポスターでは、書くことができる文字の分量がとても少ない。その中で、内容を精査しなくてはならないが、言いたいことや流れなどは維持しなくてはならない。

⑤ **セクションごとに見出しを付ける**

導入、結論などのセクションごとに見出しを付け、文字を大きめにする。

⑥ **読む順番を明白に**

見る人が、どの順番で読むのかが分かりやすいように、番号を付けたり、上から下、左から右に配列したりと工夫をする。

⑦ **レイアウト、フォント、色などが大事**

見る人が全体の流れを把握しやすいようにレイアウトを工夫する。また、小さすぎるフォント、見えにくい色、色の使い過ぎなどに気を付ける。文字は大き目で。強調したい部分のデザインを工夫する。テーマカラーを決め、色を統一する。

⑧ **図やグラフを活用しよう**

視覚に訴える図やグラフは、一目でたくさんの内容や情報を提供できるため効果的である。文字は少なく、図やイラストを多用する。また、図やグラフの要点も付加する。

例）Women Deliver（https://womendeliver.org）より

INVEST IN GIRLS' EQUALITY

THE AVERAGE LIFE EXPECTANCY FOR WOMEN:

82 YEARS IN **HIGH-INCOME** COUNTRIES

63.1 YEARS IN **LOW-INCOME** COUNTRIES

64% OF ILLITERATE ADULTS ARE WOMEN.

{ THAT'S 2 OUT OF 3 }

Girls and women spend **90%** of their **earned income on their families,** while men spend only 30-40%

VIOLENCE

ONE IN FOUR WOMEN **is physically or sexually abused during pregnancy.**

Globally, **NEARLY 40%** of murders of women are committed by an intimate partner.

EVERY DAY, 39,000 GIRLS ARE FORCED INTO EARLY MARRIAGE.

THAT'S 27 GIRLS A MINUTE

INCLUSION & PARTICIPATION

Women make up only **22%** of Parliamentarian seats, and **8%** of the world's executives.

95% of countries have a male head of state.

WOMEN IN POWER = GREATER OPPORTUNITIES FOR GIRLS' EDUCATION, HEALTH, AND EQUALITY

フWOMEN DELIVER

WHO WINS? **EVERYBODY.**

グロサリー　Glossary

Unit 1

【Page 8】
population　人口
extreme　極度の
poverty　貧困
sub-Saharan Africa　サハラ以南のアフリカ
undernourished　栄養不良の
obese　肥満の
eradicate　根絶する、撲滅させる
sanitation　公衆衛生、下水設備
underweight　低体重の
disaster　災害、天災
malnutrition　栄養不良、悪い栄養状態
stunted　発育阻害、発育停止
orphanage　児童養護施設

【Page 9】
billion　10億
middle-income　中間所得層の

【Page 10】
crucial　極めて重要［重大］な
decline　減る、減少する
estimate　見積もる、推定する
due to ...　…が原因で、…に起因して
degradation　低下、劣化、悪化
conflict　紛争
drought　干ばつ、渇水
overweight　太り過ぎの
small-scale farmer　小規模［零細］農家
encourage　勧める、奨励する
sustainable　持続できる
agriculture　農業
productivity　生産性
cooperation　連携
establish　設置［開設］する
investment　投資
infrastructure　基盤、インフラ、生活の基盤となる施設

【Page 11】
dispose　捨てる［廃棄する、処分する］
damaged packaging　損傷した容器
edible　食べられる
substantial　十分な

Food bank　フード・バンク、食糧銀行（困窮者や、困窮者に食料援助を行うNPO団体に食料を配給する、民間の組織またはその施設）
surplus　余剰
distribute　～を分配する
women's shelters　女性のための一時的な収容施設
welfare　福祉事業
beneficiary　恩恵を受ける人、受益者
donor　寄贈者、贈与者
recipient　受領者、受益者
donate　寄付する
corporate social responsibility (CSR)
　　　企業の社会的責任
expense　費用、出費
afford　～を買う［雇う・支払う］ことができる

【Page 12】
financial support　資金援助
be liable to ...　…しがちだ
trap　陥れる、抜け出せなくなる
burden　負担、重荷
chronic　習慣的な、常習的な、慢性の

Unit 2

【Page 14】
ensure　～を確かにする、保証する
promote　促進させる
well-being　健康で安心なこと、幸福
inadequate　不十分な、不適切な
hygiene　衛生状態
mortality　死亡率
fatal　命に関わる、致命的な
facility　施設、設備、機関
preventable　回避［予防］可能な
hygienic　衛生的な
infectious　感染性の
infection　感染
contribute　原因の一つになる

【Page 15】
be likely to ...　…しそうである、起こり得る
suicide　自殺
measles　はしか、麻疹
malaria　マラリア
maternal　母親の

attendant　（医療現場などでの）世話人、看護人
prevent　〈病気・事故など〉を予防する、防止する
avoid　避ける
prematurely　通常より早く

【Page 16】
newborn　新生児（の）
complication　複雑な［困難な］事態
pregnancy　妊娠
childbirth　出産
appropriate　適切な、妥当な、ふさわしい
personnel　職員、社員
contributor　原因となるもの
air pollution　大気汚染
fuel　燃料
traffic　交通（量）
power-generation　発電
waste-burning　廃棄物燃焼
residential　居住の
disorder　疾患
anxiety　不安、心配、懸念
depression　落ち込み
life expectancy　平均余命（ある年齢の人があと何年生きら
　　れるかの統計的期待値）

【Page 17】
diarrhea　下痢
pneumonia　肺炎
dispenser　ディスペンサー（紙タオル〔コップ〕、液体石けん
　　などを必要量ずつ取り出せる容器）
severe　厳しい、深刻な、重大な
awareness　〔あるものについて〕気付いて［自覚して］いること

【Page 18】
stillbirth　死産
strategic　方策の、方略の
morbidity　病的な状態、罹病率

Unit 3

【Page 20】
inclusive　包摂的な、すべての人々を含む
equitable　公平な、公正な
adolescent　青年、若者
proficiency　技能、能力
illiterate　非識字の、読み書きができない
compulsory　必須の、義務の
enrolment　入学、就学
literacy　識字、読み書きの能力
remote　遠い、遠隔の

【Page 21】
considerable　かなりの、相当の
participation　参加

【Page 22】
inequality　不平等、不公平、不均衡
foster　育成する、促進する
tolerance　寛容、包容力
differ　異なる
martial arts　武道、格闘技
citizenship　市民権、市民意識

【Page 23】
statistics　統計
out-of-school　通学していない
attend　出席する
deprive ~ of ...　～から…を奪う
motivation　動機、やる気
stationery　文具
household　家計
attitude　態度、姿勢、考え方

【Page 24】
invest　投資する
purchase　購入する
laptop　ノートパソコン（「ノートパソコン」は和製英語）

Unit 4

【Page 26】
gender　ジェンダー、社会的・文化的観点から見た性差
equality　平等、等しいこと、同等（のもの）
empower　～に力をつけさせる、～に能力を与える
unpaid　無給の、無報酬の
domestic　家庭の、家事の
income　所得、収入
household　家庭、世帯、一家
neuter　中性の、無性の
decision-making　意思決定
unpaid work　無償労働、ただ働き
discrimination　不公平な扱い、差別
socio-economic　社会経済の、社会経済的な
duty-free　無税（の）、免税（の）
migrant　移住者、移民、移住性の

【Page 27】
ever-partnered　これまでパートナーがいたことがある
underrepresented　過少に少なく・低く評価する
representation　代表［代理］を務めること
parliament　国会、議会
LDCs　後発開発途上国（= the Least Developed Countries）

low-income　低所得の

【Page 28】
enormous　非常に大きな、巨大な
drive up　つり上げる、跳ね上がらせる
decent work　働きがいのある人間らしい仕事
segregation　分離、隔離（人種・宗教・性別などによって人々の居場所を別々に分けること）
wage gap　賃金格差
landmark agreement　画期的な合意
billionaire　億万長者
fetch　〔物や人を〕取り［連れ］に行ってくる、取って［連れて］くる
firewood　まき
responsibility　責任、義務

【Page 29】
Taliban　タリバン（イスラム原理主義組織）
regime　政治［統治］体制
investment　投資
co-founded　共同で設立した
mitigate　和らげる、緩和する
humanitarian　人道主義

【Page 30】
devastating　破壊的な、衝撃的な

【Page 31】
gender bias　社会的・文化的性差による偏見、性差［ジェンダー］に関する先入観
prosperity　繁盛

Unit 5

【Page 32】
reduced　削減［縮小］された
recurring　繰り返し起きる
shortage　〔〜の〕不足
human waste　人糞
irrigation　かんがい
open defecation　屋外での排便

【Page 33】
scarcity　不足
contaminated　汚染された
thoroughly　完全に

【Page 34】
human right　人権
fecally　糞便によって
supply　供給

hygiene practice　衛生習慣
flush toilet　水洗トイレ

【Page 35】
durable　耐久性のある
combat　〜と闘う、〜に対抗する
living standard　生活水準
predict　〜を予測する
groundwater　地下水
adapt　順応［適応・変化］させる

【Page 36】
decent　適切な
end up …　結局［最後には］…になる
valuable　役立つ

Unit 6

【Page 38】
electricity　電気、電力
mostly　主に
obtain　取得する、入手する
consumption　消費、飲食、食物摂取
source　源
affordable　手頃な価格、入手可能な
renewable　再生可能な
carbon dioxide　二酸化炭素
pollute　〜を汚染する
alternative　代替手段［案］
replenish　補充する
emission　排出
hydroelectricity　水力電気
geothermal　地熱の
biomass　バイオマス（代替エネルギーの供給源としての植物）

【Page 39】
clean energy　クリーンエネルギー
coal　石炭
mustard gas　マスタード・ガス（第1次大戦中に化学兵器として使われた。皮膚と粘膜をびらんさせ、致命的な呼吸困難を引き起こすことがある）
kerosene　灯油
approximately　おおよそ
unplug　プラグを抜いて電気を切る
appliance　電化製品、設備
obstacle　障害（物）、妨害（物）、邪魔

【Page 40】
greenhouse gas　温室効果ガス
livelihood　生活
device　機器

efficient　効率的な
fossil fuel　化石燃料
constantly　何度も
generate　〜を作り出す
massive　大量の
waterfall　滝
animal manure　動物のふん（の肥料）
sewage　下水、汚水
convert　転換する

【Page 41】
pellet stove　ペレットストーブ
principle　動作［作用］原理
densify　〜を圧縮する
sawdust　おがくず
forestry residue　森林廃棄物
dump　投げ捨てる
landfill　埋め立てごみ（処理地）、ごみ廃棄場
absorb　吸収する
carbon neutral　カーボンニュートラル（植物由来の原料の場合、燃やして炭酸ガスを放出しても、その炭酸ガス中の炭素は元来植物が光合成によって大気中の炭酸ガスから取り込んだものなので、大気中の炭酸ガス濃度は常に一定に保たれる。このような炭素循環の考え方をカーボンニュートラルという）
combustion　燃焼
exhaust　使い果たす
decompose　腐敗［腐食］させる、分解する
toxic　有毒な
ignition　点火、着火
power modulation　電力変調
install　設置する

【Page 42】
reliable　信頼［信用］できる
feed-in tariff　固定価格買取制度（自然エネルギーの普及などのため、買取価格を法律で定め、助成する制度）
LNG　液化天然ガス（＝ liquefied natural gas）
respectively　それぞれ、各々
scale back　規模を縮小する
expansion　拡大

Unit 7

【Page 44】
inclusive　包括的な
child labor　児童労働
significant　重要な
earnings　報酬、賃金
opportunity　良い機会、好機
vocational　職業の、職業教育の

engage in ...　…に従事する、…に携わる

【Page 46】
rooted　根付いた、根のある
label 〜 as ...　〜に…という表示を付ける、〜を…に分類する、〜に…というレッテルを貼る
forced labor　強制労働
hazardous　有害な、危険な
endanger　〜を危険にさらす、危うくする

【Page 47】
pesticide　殺虫剤
scale　規模
victim　被害者
human trafficking　人身売買
monitor　監視する、観察する
convey　伝える
mobilize　動員する
enroll　登録する、入学させる

Unit 8

【Page 50】
innovation　革新、刷新
infrastructure　社会基盤、インフラ
resilient　強靭な、回復力のある
industrialization　産業化、工業化
manufacture　製造業
material　材料、素材
investment　投資
profit　利益
microcredit　マイクロクレジット（貧困層の人々を対象とした少額融資）
exploit　搾取する
unfairly　不公平に

【Page 51】
manufacturing value added (MVA)　製造業付加価値（製品を製造し販売した際の売上高から原材料等の購入費を引いたもの）
per capita　〈ラテン語〉《統計》一人当たりの
challenge　困難な問題、難問
lines of credit　融資限度、最大貸付金額
dispatching　派遣
in contrast　対照的に
handicrafts　工芸（品）、手芸（品）
heavy metal　重金属
mining　採鉱、鉱業
public transportation　公共交通
cellular phone　携帯電話

【Page 52】
deforestation　森林伐採、森林破壊
instability　不安定（さ）
resident　住人、居住者
disparity　格差
scarce　乏しい、欠乏した
can't afford to ...　…する（金銭的）余裕がない

【Page 53】
collateral　担保
interest　利子、利息
repay　払い戻す、返済する
implement　実行する、実施する
attain　得る、達成する
criteria　標準、基準（単数形は criterion）

【Page 54】
impose　課す、負わせる

【Page 55】
nominal　名目の
hypothesis　仮説
diffusion　普及、拡散
correlate　相互に関係がある、相関する

Unit 9

【Page 56】
urban　都市の、都会の
slum　貧民街、スラム
unwanted　求められていない、不必要な
disposal　廃棄、処理
vehicle　乗り物
vulnerable　弱い、脆弱な
potential　潜在的な、ありうる
exacerbate　悪化させる
jeopardize　危険にさらす
hand-to-mouth　その日暮らしの、一時しのぎの

【Page 57】
breathe　呼吸する

【Page 58】
spatial　空間の、場所の
mandate　権限を委託する
address　取り組む、対処する、働きかける
collaborative　共同（協働）の
immediate　即時の
densely　密集して
coronavirus　コロナウイルス
overcrowding　（人の）密集、過密

social distancing　物理的距離
self-isolation　自己隔離

【Page 59】
coral reef　サンゴ礁
overflow　あふれる
color-coded　色分けされた

【Page 60】
neglect　怠る、疎かにする、無視する
fertilizer　肥料
informal　非公式の
urbanization　都市化
catalyst　触媒、促進するもの

Unit 10

【Page 62】
energy efficient　エネルギー［資源］効率の良い
litter　ごみ
biodegradable　生（物）分解可能な
decay　腐る
ecological footprint　エコロジカル・フットプリント（人間
　　が生きていくために使用している自然環境［農地・牧場・漁
　　獲海域・森林などの生態系リソース］の総面積）
CO_2 emission　CO_2［二酸化炭素］排出量
livestock　家畜

【Page 63】
lightbulb　電球
wheat　小麦
multiply　〜を拡大させる
cut down　削減する、減らす

【Page 64】
consume　消費する
profound　深刻な
marine life　海洋生物
washed-up　疲れ切った
pollution　汚染
for generations　何世代にもわたり［わたって］

【Page 65】
rely on ...　…を頼り［当て］にする
along with ...　…と併せて
purify　〜を浄化する
protein　タンパク質

【Page 66】
rubbish　ごみ、廃棄物
refer to ...　…に言及する

electronic 電子的な
utility 有用性
redundancy 余剰性
breakage 破損

Unit 11

【Page 68】
urgent 緊急の、差し迫った
concentration 濃度
pre-industrial level 産業革命前［以前］の
mean temperature 平均温度［気温］
sea level 海水面、海水位
extinction （動植物の種族の）絶滅
emit 放つ、放射する
melt 溶ける、融解する
flooding 洪水、氾濫
deplete 使い果たす［尽くす］

【Page 70】
driver 原動力、けん引役
escape 逃げる
solid waste 固形廃棄物
burp げっぷ
nitrous oxide 亜酸化窒素
manure （有機質）肥料、肥やし
residue 残留物
chlorofluorocarbon フロンガス
ice sheet （北極・南極を覆う）氷床
erosion 浸食
proliferate 急増する
crop 作物、農作物

【Page 71】
divestment （子会社や株などの）売却、処分
stock 株、株式
bond 保証証券
fund 国債、公債
pension fund 年金基金
investment capital 投下［投資］資本
implication 意味あい
take action 行動を取る［起こす］
trillion 1兆
withdraw 引き落とす
drastically 大幅に

【Page 72】
steadily 着実に
aviation 航空

Unit 12

【Page 74】
conserve 保存する、保護する、保全する
restore ～を元の状態に戻す、～を修復［復元・復旧］する
terrestrial 地球の、陸地の
ecosystem 生態系
desertification 砂漠化
biodiversity 生物の種が多様であること、種［生態系］の
　　多様性、生物学的多様性、生物の多種多様性
fish stock 魚種資源
overfish 魚を乱獲する
be equivalent to 同じ、同等の、同意義の
habitat 生息環境、生息地、生息場所、居住環境、居住地

【Page 75】
global warming 地球温暖化
tropical rainforest 熱帯雨林

【Page 76】
surface 表面、面
oxygen 酸素
regulate 調整する、調節する
atmosphere 大気
freshwater 真水
species 種
moderately ほどほどに、適度に

【Page 77】
nutritious 栄養になる、滋養の多い
threaten ～の［する］恐れがある、～の兆候を示す
impair 悪くする、損なう、害する、減じる、弱める
illegal 違法の
unreported 報告されていない
unregulated 規制［規定・統制・管理・制限・調節・調整］
　　されていない、無秩序な

【Page 78】
wildlife 野生動物
eliminate 除外する
spoil 台無しになる、だめになる、腐る、役に立たなくなる
intake 摂取量

Unit 13

【Page 80】
accountable 責任がある、責任を持つ
at all levels あらゆる水準［レベル］で
detect 見つける、検知する
trafficking 不法な取引、密売
verify 確かめる

defender 擁護者
trade unionist 労働組合員、労働組合主義者
persecution 迫害
homicide 殺人
refugee 難民、避難民
exploitation 搾取
abduct 誘拐する

【Page 81】
flee 逃げる、逃れる

【Page 82】
civil war 内戦
shelter 住居
national human rights institution (NHRI) 国内人権機関（政府から独立した、人権の促進・擁護を目的として各国に設置される機関）
the Paris Principles パリ原則（1993年に国連総会で決議された「国内人権機関の地位に関する原則」の通称。各国に国内人権機関 (NHRI) の設置を求めている）
resolve 決議する
assembly 集会、総会

【Page 83】
recruit 募集する、（新兵を）集める
armed 武装した
servant 使用人、召し使い
resistance 抵抗
Lord's Resistance Army (LRA) 神の抵抗軍（ウガンダおよびその周辺で活動する反政府組織）
brainwash 洗脳する
acceptance 受容、受け入れ
psychotherapy 精神療法、心理療法
trauma 精神的外傷、トラウマ

【Page 84】
kidnap 誘拐する
extremist 過激主義者
awful 恐ろしい、ひどい
exceed 超える、超過する
forcibly 強制的に
displace 立ち退かせる、退去させる

【Page 85】
geographical 地理的な

Unit 14

【Page 86】
implementation 遂行、実施
revitalize ～を復興させる、再生する

hosting refugees 難民受け入れ
digital divide 情報（技術）格差（によって生じる経済格差）
remittance 送金
private sector 民間部門［企業］
net 正味の、最終的な
ODA 政府開発援助 (= Official Development Assistance)
public-private partnership (PPP) 官民［公共と民間］のパートナーシップ

【Page 87】
multilateral aid 多国間援助
flow （資金・現金・情報などの）流れ
be projected to ... …すると予測される
South-South cooperation 南南協力（開発途上国による別の開発途上国への支援）
hemisphere 半球

【Page 88】
commitment 公約、献身、約束、深い関与
coherent 理路整然と［首尾一貫］していて分かりやすい
critical 重要な、重大な
accountability 説明責任［義務］
devise 考案［立案］する
initiative 新たな取り組み、イニシアティブ
launch 始める
general assembly 総会、全体会、国連総会

【Page 89】
long-term 長期間にわたる
public sector 公営企業、公的部門
financial crisis 経営［金融・財政的］危機
qualitatively 定性的に
quantitatively 定量的に
Private Finance Initiative 民間資金主導（政府が景気対策として、公共事業を積極的に民間企業に委託しようとすること）
numerous 多数の、非常に多くの
concession 特権、利権
imminent 差し迫った
prevalent 流行［普及・まん延］している
foster ～を発展させる、～を育成する

【Page 90】
proactively 前向きに、積極的に
physician 医師
necessarily （否定形で）必ずしも～でない
firm 確固たる
philosophy 哲学
perspective 視点
offline オフラインで

CLIL 英語で考えるＳＤＧｓ
―持続可能な開発目標

2021 年 2 月 20 日　第 1 版発行
2024 年 3 月 10 日　第 15 版発行

著　　者——笹島　茂（ささじま　しげる）

　　　　　　小島さつき（こじま　さつき）

　　　　　　安部由紀子（あべ　ゆきこ）

　　　　　　佐藤元樹（さとう　もとき）

　　　　　　Barry Kavanagh（ばりー　かばなー）

　　　　　　工藤泰三（くどう　たいぞう）

発 行 者——前田俊秀

発 行 所——株式会社 三修社

　　　　　　〒 150-0001 東京都渋谷区神宮前 2-2-22
　　　　　　TEL03-3405-4511　FAX03-3405-4522
　　　　　　振替 00190-9-72758
　　　　　　https://www.sanshusha.co.jp
　　　　　　編集担当　永尾真理

印 刷 所——日経印刷株式会社

表紙デザイン —— 岩泉卓屋
本文 DTP　 —— 川原田良一

文法マスター

CLIL
Content & Language Integrated Learning

SDGs
Sustainable Development Goals

Shigeru Sasajima

Satsuki Kojima

Yukiko Abe

Motoki Sato

Barry Kavanagh

Taizo Kudo

SANSHUSHA

Unit 1

現在形
present simple

現在形は、「習慣的に昨日も今日も明日も繰り返し行われること」と「事実」に関して使われます。頻度を表す副詞とともに扱われる場合は、ふつう副詞＋一般動詞、be 動詞＋副詞の語順となります。

❶習慣的に繰り返し行われること（例えば、学校へ行く、歯を磨くなど）

例 A lot of people still **live** on less than US$1.90 a day.

一日 1.9 ドル以下で生活している人がいるという状態を表す。

❷事実（例えば、太陽は東から昇る、水は 100 度で沸騰するなど）

例 Half of all people living in poverty **are** usually under 18.

貧しい国で暮らしている人の半分が 18 歳以下だという事実を表す。

【問題を解いてみよう！】次の単語を並べ替えなさい。

1) people / health care / have / to / poor / adequate / usually / do not / access

_____

2) a food bank / in / never / 80 % / food / of people / poverty / access

_____

3) agriculture / several / all over / small-scale / faces / problems / the world

_____

4) drought / food / associated / serious / shortage / with / often / is

_____

5) generations / poor families / poor / remain / for / three or more

_____

Unit 2

接続詞
conjunctions

and, but, or などの等位接続詞は、対等な関係にある語と語、句と句、節と節を結びつけます。また、特にライティングでは、文のはじめに and, but, so を使用することは避け、代わりに transition words（転換語）などを使いましょう。

❶対等な関係

例 It is important **not only** to be vaccinated, **but also** to follow good hygiene practice.

❷転換語の例

and:	also, in addition
but:	however, on the other hand
so:	therefore, as a result

例 Handwashing is effective to prevent infectious diseases. However, the rate of handwashing is low in many countries.

【問題を解いてみよう！】 適切な接続詞を用いて、次の2つの文をつなげなさい。

1) Mortality rates have been reduced. Life expectancy continues to increase globally.

_____

2) It is crucial to reduce maternal mortality. It is crucial to reduce stillbirths.

_____

3) Funding for malaria had been increasing since 2000. It has recently decreased.

_____

4) Air pollution increases the risk of disease. It leads to millions of deaths every year.

_____

5) Half of the world's population suffers from financial hardship. They are still without access to essential health services.

_____

2

Unit 3 現在進行形
present progressive

現在進行形は「現在進行中の動作や継続」、「確実な未来」そして「状況や物事の変化」といった意味を表すときに使います。また、進行形でふつう使用しない動詞（want, like, belong, know, suppose, remember, forget, understand, need, realize, mean, forget, believe など）に注意しましょう。

❶現在進行中の動作や出来事、動作の反復、一定の期間内の習慣などを表します。

例 I **am studying** about the SDGs at the moment.

今を含めた一定期間内（最近）に SDGs を勉強していることを表す。

❷確定された未来や予定に向かって進んでいることを表します。

例 I **am donating** the money to the poor schools this weekend.

確定された未来（今週末）に、貧しい学校にお金を寄付する予定であることを表す。

❸状況や物事の変化を表す表現として使われます。

例 The population of the world **is rising** very fast.

世界人口の増加現象を示しているということを表す。

【問題を解いてみよう！】 単語を利用し、今現在起きていることを表すように文を作りなさい。

1) government programs / improve / the situation / for the poor children

_____

2) Latin American communities / bridge / the skills gap

_____

3) the city / promote / quality education

_____

4) African children / face / a future of unemployment / and poverty

_____

5) girls / suffer from / discrimination / based on their gender

_____

過去形・過去進行形
past simple and past progressive

動詞の過去形は、過去に完結した行為や、過去の習慣的出来事を表します。過去のある特定の時に進行していた動作や継続していた状態を表すときには、過去進行形（was/were と動詞の -ing 形）を使います。

❶ **過去の出来事の最中に別の出来事が起きていた場合、過去進行形が when 節や while 節とともに使われます。**

例 <u>While</u> most of the girls in developed countries **were enjoying** school life, many girls in other countries still **had** to work.

❷ **過去の出来事が同時に進行していない場合は、過去形を使いましょう。**

例 After their husbands **came** back home, most women in developing countries **prepared** a meal.

= Their husbands **came** back home, and then most women in developing countries **prepared** a meal.

【問題を解いてみよう！】与えられた動詞を適切な形にして文を完成させなさい。

1) The world is a better place for women today than it (　　　　　) in the past.
   `be`

2) Globally, around 750 million of women alive today (　　　　　) married before their 18th birthday.　`be`

3) At a time when Sara was promoted to a managerial position, Kinbari, a girl living in a developing country, (　　　　　) to get married before her 18th birthday.
   `prepare`

4) All female who (　　　　　) child marriage didn't have formal employment irrespective of their school status.　`experience`

5) While women (　　　　　) 39 percent of world employment, only 27 percent of managerial positions in the world were occupied by women.　`represent`

助動詞
auxiliary verbs

助動詞は、話し手の気持ちや態度を表し、自分（話し手）の意見や考えを伝えるとき、文の主語の意志・能力・義務を表すときに使います。助動詞の後では動詞は原形です。

❶ 自分（話し手）の考えや気持ちを伝える表現

should：何かよい考えや解決策を提案するとき

例 You **should** not waste water in your daily life.

日常生活で水を無駄使いすべきでないという話し手の考えを示す。

could：可能な解決策を提案するとき

例 You **could** use waste to create art.

ゴミでアート作品を作ることができるかもしれないという話し手の考えを示す。

❷ 文の主語の意志、能力、義務を表すとき

例 Some **can** play with water, but others **have to** drink dirty water.

水で遊ぶことができる人がいるが、汚れた水を飲まなければならない人もいるという話し手の考えを表す。

【問題を解いてみよう！】空欄に適切な助動詞を入れて文を完成させなさい。

1) Wasted water（　　　　　　　　）be seen as a sustainable source of water rather than as a burden.

2) Drinking water（　　　　　　　　）be affordable, which means that payment for services should not prevent access to clean water.

3) By 2030, 700 million people（　　　　　　　　）be displaced by intense water scarcity.

4) Around 670 million people still（　　　　　　　　）practice open defecation.

5) 5.2 billion people（　　　　　　　　）access basic drinking water, but 785 million people cannot.

Unit 6 形容詞・副詞
adjectives and adverbs

形容詞は、名詞を修飾し、補語としても働きます。副詞は、副詞、動詞、形容詞を修飾します。

❶形容詞 (-able, -ful, -ant, -al, -ive, -tic など) は名詞を修飾します。

　例 extremely **important** fuel

❷形容詞は、補語の働きもします。

　例 Sustainable energy is **important**.

❸副詞 (-ly) は、副詞、形容詞、動詞を修飾します。

　例 High-level Political Forum on Sustainable Development meets **annually**.

　　We have **recently** received investment and support from the government.

【問題を解いてみよう！】適切な語を選びなさい。

1) Fossil fuel is creating (drastic / drastically) changes to our climate.

2) By investing in solar energy, you can (ultimately / ultimate) save money.

3) Let's find ways to use energy (effectively / effective / effectivity) in buildings.

4) 3 billion people rely on polluting and (unhealthiness / unhealthy) fuels for cooking.

5) Energy is central to (nearly / near / neared) every major challenge the world faces today.

6) The use of renewable (electric / electrical / electricity) is increasing in the world.

7) Greenhouse gases have a (harm / harmful / harmfully) impact on people's well-being.

分詞
participles

分詞は、形容詞と同じように、名詞を修飾したり、述語として使用されたりします。完了や受身の意味では、過去分詞（動詞の -ed 形）を使い、未完了や進行の意味では、現在分詞（動詞の -ing 形）を使いましょう。

❶名詞の修飾語句として

　・過去分詞

　例 **developed** countries（先進国）

　・現在分詞

　例 **developing** countries（開発途上国）

❷ be 動詞の後に述語として

　例 There is no clear agreement on which country is **developed** or which country is **developing**.

【問題を解いてみよう！】与えられた語句を用いて、文を完成させなさい。

【employed / unemployed / educated / increasing /
living / developed / developing / continued】

1) The number of (　　　　　　　　) people is rapidly increasing every year.

2) (　　　　　　　　) people have more employment opportunities.

3) A(n) (　　　　　　　　) number of young people are neither participating in education and training nor employed.

4) The number of workers (　　　　　　　　) in extreme poverty has declined dramatically.

5) Many (　　　　　　) countries are looking for ways to ensure (　　　　　　　　) growth.

6) Women in (　　　　　　　　) countries are more often (　　　　　　　　) in lower-wage and low skilled jobs than men.

Unit 8 主語と動詞の一致
subject-verb agreement

主語が単数か複数かによって、動詞の形態が変わってきます。主語が単数なら動詞も単数の形に、主語が複数なら動詞も複数の形になります。また、主語と動詞は、人称や時制を一致させる原則があります。

❶ government, staff, family, team, committee などの集合名詞は、複数扱いとなります。

例 More than 4 billion **people** still **do** not have access to the Internet.

*people は、それを組織している個々の人を表すため複数形。

❷ 主語に every, each, either, neither が含まれると単数扱いとなります。

例 **Each** of us **has** the power to confront the issues of SDGs.

❸ someone, somebody, something, anyone, anybody, anything, everything, every one, nobody, no one, nothing は、単数扱いとなります。

例 **Nobody wants** to feel left out.

【問題を解いてみよう！】適切な動詞を選びなさい。

1) Everyone (want / wants) to help their family, their community, their country.

2) People (need / needs) access to the Internet.

3) There (is / are) someone somewhere moving the SDGs forward.

4) Children (is / are) by nature more vulnerable than adults.

5) Each of the goals (is / are) connected to each other.

Unit 9 関係代名詞
relative pronouns

関係詞代名詞は、形容詞のように名詞を修飾し、補足説明するはたらきをします。何を修飾するのかによって、関係代名詞の形が変わります。

❶ 人を修飾するときは、その後に、関係代名詞 who（that）を使います。
people と関係詞節内の動詞 live に数の一致があることに注意しましょう。

例 *People* **who** live in cities are breathing polluted air.

［都市に住んでいる］人々は汚染された空気を吸っているということを表す。

❷ 人ではないものを修飾するときは、その後に、関係代名詞 which（that）を使います。
ここでも air と関係詞節内の be 動詞に数の一致があることに注意しましょう

例 Urban residents are breathing *air* **which** is polluted.

都市住民は［汚染された］空気を吸っているということを表す。

【問題を解いてみよう！】
次のチャート内の語句と関係詞節を使って、事実を表す文を完成させなさい。

people half of people	live in urban areas live in slums	do not have soap and water are exposed to air pollution have convenient access to public transport lack access to basic services and housing

1)

　

2)

　

3)

　

4)

Unit 10 関係副詞 relative adverbs

関係副詞は、前の名詞（先行詞）の場所 (where)、時 (when)、理由 (why) について説明を加える際に使用します。前置詞＋関係代名詞についても確認しましょう。

❶ Landfills where garbage is buried under the soil will be full soon.
    ← Landfills will be full soon ＋ garbage is buried under the soil in the landfills
landfill を説明している後ろの文と前の文を、where でくっつけています。また、後ろの文で、landfill が副詞として働いている（前置詞が必要）。
    ＝ Landfills in which garbage is buried... とも言える。

❷ The time when all the SDGs targets are accomplished will come.
    ← The time will come ＋ all the SDGs targets are accomplished at the time.
    ＝ The time at which all the SDGs targets will be ... とも言える。

❸ We need to find the reason why humans consume too many resources.
    *why は reason が先行詞の時のみに使われるため省略されることもある。

【問題を解いてみよう！】次の二つの文を一文に書き換えなさい。

1) Do you know the reason? We need to reduce our ecological footprint for this reason.

_____

2) It is the time. We shift towards a more resource efficient economy at the time.

_____

3) The food is provided to some people at the food bank. The food bank is the place.

_____

4) There are some cases. Doubting common sense will lead you to find the best idea for SDGs in some cases.

_____

Unit 11 動名詞・不定詞
gerunds and infinitives

動名詞 (-ing) と不定詞 (to) は、名詞の働きをします。動詞によって、動名詞のみ、不定詞のみ、または、その両方を取るか異なります。

❶動名詞のみをとる動詞は、現在または過去の経験・行為への指向があります。

admit, consider, suggest, avoid, involve, deny, give up, keep, go on など

例 It is important to **keep talking** about climate change.

❷不定詞のみを取る動詞は、未来 (これからのこと) への指向があります。

want, agree, offer, decide, hope, promise, expect, learn, tend, seem など

例 We **want to learn** about climate change and its effects.

❸動名詞と不定詞のどちらでも構わない動詞があります。

like, love, start, prefer, hate, begin, continue など

例 Do you **like to use / using** public transportation?

❹動名詞・不定詞の両方を取る動詞で、それぞれ意味が異なる場合があります。

stop, remember, need, try など

例 We **need to understand** climate change.

理解する必要がある

例 Climate change **needs understanding**.

理解される必要がある

【問題を解いてみよう！】 与えられた動詞を動名詞か不定詞にして、空欄に補いなさい。

1) It's clear that we should avoid (　　　　　　) fossil fuels as much as possible.
   use

2) My university decided (　　　　　　) renewable energy technologies.　install

3) Some countries have stopped (　　　　　) new nuclear powerplants.
   introduce

4) As the planet warms, scientists expect (　　　　　　) big ecological changes in
   the Arctic.　see

5) Twelve out of the 17 SDGs involve (　　　　　　) action on climate change.
   take

Unit 12 比較 comparatives

-er/more を用いた形容詞や副詞の形は、単に物事を比較するときだけでなく、物事の変化や量の増減を表すときにも使用されます。名詞に more をつけるときは、可算名詞では複数形 (more) animals に、不可算名詞はそのまま単数形 (more) fish にします。

❶形容詞の比較級

例 The ocean is **larger** than the entire land area on the earth.

❷副詞の比較級

例 Biodiversity is declining **faster** than at any other time in human history.

❸ 名詞の比較級

例 **More animals** are being pushed out of their natural habitats.
The world now farms **more fish** than it catches.

【問題を解いてみよう！】 与えられた形容詞や名詞を適切な形に直して、空欄に補い文を完成させなさい。

1) Wild fish stocks are declining (　　　　　　　　) than we thought.　fast

2) The Amazon forest regrows much (　　　　　　　　) than first thought.　slow

3) We're losing more (　　　　　　) than we're planting.　tree

4) The oceans will have (　　　　　　) than fish.　plastic

5) The problem of plastic in the ocean is (　　　　　　　) than we thought.　bad

6) In forest management, sustainability means not to cut down (　　　　　　　) than will grow back.　wood

Unit 13 冠詞 articles

基本的に名詞には冠詞 (a/an, the) が付きます。初めて話題に上る単数形の可算名詞には不定冠詞 a/an(特定できない中の一つ) が付き、すでに話し手・聞き手双方に認識されている名詞には定冠詞 the（すでにわかっているもの、特定のもの、場所など）が付きます。日本語にはない文法なので確認しましょう。

例 There is **an** interesting SNS campaign. **The** campaign is about preventing violent extremism.

初めて話題に上がる campaign には不定冠詞 (a/an) が付き、「ある campaign」となり、もうすでに話題に上がっている次の campaign には定冠詞 (the) がつき、「その campaign」となっている。

【問題を解いてみよう！】適切な冠詞を選びなさい。

1) Armed violence has (a / the) destructive impact on a country's development.

2) In some countries, (a / the) child's legal proof of identity is missing. Without (a / the) legal proof, many children can't get routine vaccines and other healthcare services.

3) Human trafficking is (a /the) crime that forcefully exploits women, men, and children. (A / The) victims of crime are mainly women and girls.

4) Every week, (an / the) average of nine people were murdered. (An / The) average is increasing every year.

5) There has been (an / the) overall increase in (a / the) detection of victims of trafficking, which could reflect either (a / the) positive or negative development.

6) There is (an / the) armed group called LRA. (A / The) boy called "Charles" was abducted by (a / the) group ten years ago.

直接話法・間接話法
direct and reported speech

直接話法の形で、誰かの発言をそのまま引用するときには、quotation marks（引用符）" "を用います（主に英国では single quotation marks ' ' が用いられます）。間接話法は、内容を伝えます。引用符を使うときは、カンマ (,) や疑問符 (?) の位置に注意しましょう。

❶間接話法から直接話法への転換

例 He said (that) we needed strong collaboration with government, corporations, communities, academia and other organizations.

・He said, "We need strong collaboration with … and other organization."

・"We need strong collaboration with … and other organization," he said.

❷ 間接話法（間接疑問文）から直接話法への転換

例 The mayor asked if there were any questions.

・The mayor asked, "Are there any questions?"

・"Are there any questions?" the mayor asked.

【問題を解いてみよう！】間接話法は直接話法の文に、直接話法は間接話法の文に書き換えなさい。

1) "These new partnerships could lead to a fantastic increase in the well-being of people," he added.

_____

2) He asked whether the SDGs had been embedded in the mayor's plan.

_____

3) She said the government alone was unable to solve these challenges.

_____

4) The United Nations secretary said, "We are facing a global health crisis in the 75-year history of the United Nations."

_____